## Praise for *Three Colors, Twelve Notes*

"Catherine Harrison challenges the reader to be curious, to be courageous, and to let their imagination soar."

**MARY ELLEN ISKENDERIAN,** President and CEO, Women's World Banking

"A masterfully written account that connects the reader to their own sense of possibility."

**TONJA MORRIS**, Chief Human Resources Officer, Wrench Group, LLC

"Those who make a habit of looking for meaning and transformation in unusual places will enjoy this curious little book."

**BENOIT-ANTOINE BACON**, President and Vice-Chancellor, Professor of Psychology, Carleton University

"Navigating uncertainty in our lives isn't easy, and this book gives us hope and confidence to unleash our creative side."

**CAROLYN SWORA**, Workplace Culture Architect, Owner of Pinnacle Culture, and Author of *Rules of Engagement*

"All people managers—from newly minted leaders to C-suite executives—should read this book."

**DAN TAYLOR**, Executive Vice-President,
Wellington-Altus Private Wealth

"Read this book to learn how to blend those three colors and play those twelve notes your own way, for yourself, and for everyone else too."

**RICHARD SCARSBROOK**, Author of ·
Rockets Versus Gravity and many other books

"A magical set of stories that invite us to become more curious about who we are and what we may become."

**JONATHAN MALES**, PhD, Sport Psychologist,
Olympic Coach, and Masters World Champion Canoeist

"In this entertaining and inspiring book, Catherine proves the power of saying yes."

**GRANT LAWRENCE**, Radio and TV Broadcaster,
and Author of Adventures in Solitude and Dirty Windshields

# THREE COLORS,
## TWELVE NOTES

Stay curious!
Catherine

# THE ALCHEMY OF CURIOSITY, CREATIVITY, AND HUMAN-CENTERED LEADERSHIP

*Catherine Harrison*

# Three Colors, Twelve Notes

**PAGE TWO**
BOOKS

*This goes out to anyone who has yet to find their voice.*
*It's in there—keep going!*

Cataloguing in publication information is
available from Library and Archives Canada.
ISBN 978-1-77458-018-9 (paperback)
ISBN 978-1-77458-019-6 (ebook)

Page Two
www.pagetwo.com

Edited by Emily Schultz
Copyedited by Crissy Calhoun
Cover and interior design by Taysia Louie
Cover and interior art by Catherine Harrison
Additional graphics by Taysia Louie
Lyrics by Catherine Harrison

catherineharrison.com

*"Stories have to be told or they die,
and when they die, we can't remember
who we are or why we're here."*

SUE MONK KIDD,
*THE SECRET LIFE OF BEES*

# Contents

*"I wrote my first novel because
I wanted to read it."*

TONI MORRISON

# Introduction

AS THE STORY goes, when John Lennon attended one of Yoko Ono's art exhibits in 1966, he fell in love with her. Why? One of her conceptual art pieces was a stepladder leading to a small piece of canvas on the ceiling. Guests were instructed to ascend the ladder and then use the provided magnifying glass to read what they saw. As Lennon told *Rolling Stone* in 1971, "And in tiny little letters it says 'yes.' So, it was positive. I felt relieved. It's a great relief when you get up the ladder and you look through the spyglass and it doesn't say 'no' or 'fuck you' or something, it said 'yes.'" (If anyone can get away with dropping an F-bomb in the first paragraph of a book without causing offense, it's John Lennon.)

I have always loved that story. I just like all that "yes" signifies. And, as a huge Lennon and Beatles fan, I get why he would connect to that so strongly. In that tiny word, there is a universe of opportunity. There is a willingness to explore consciousness, to have cool conversations; there is both a weightiness and a weightlessness to it.

"Yes" is the basis of meaningful change, transformation, adaptation, learning, growth, adventure, self-advocacy, empowerment, compassion, innovation, embracing uncertainty, stepping into discomfort. It is necessary. It is Yes-essary. "Yes" is a catalyst.

Hello, my name is Catherine. Nice to meet you. You're probably wondering, "What do you do?"

I'm a professional coach, behavior change specialist, writer, songwriter, musician, fierce environmentalist, mother, business owner, painter, recovering corporate animal, meditator, ardent walker and roamer of paths, proud Canadian, seeker, and lifelong learner.

Yep, a whole bunch of things. (Just like you, but different!) Aren't we all just a collection of identities and roles and masks and experiences? Some we attach to more strongly than others and keep for a lifetime. Some we try on like a new pair of pants and go, "Nah, not for me, but good to know, glad I tried them on."

Wishfully, I'm middle-aged, but more likely, I've got more ground behind me than ahead of me. As time spins ever faster, I want to ensure I'm taking full and regular advantage of the notions of adapting and transforming and thriving. Whether I'm on a stage or having a conversation, walking through nature, or experimenting with artistic materials, at the heart of it my whole life is about connecting, creating, and communicating.

I've been reflecting on how curiosity has shaped my journey so far, how it has opened me up to experiences and expansion and opportunity to meet people, go places, and learn things. How leveraging and cultivating a lifelong focus on adapting and learning and growing and evolving has brought me countless riches. And I don't mean money. That's just one form of currency. Riches manifest as various energies—currencies—that we are constantly exchanging. Riches manifest in the smallest and simplest ways. Even in the difficult times. In sharing this collection of reflections, my intention is to invite you to use your own curiosity and creativity to examine your life and to make meaningful choices and meaningful changes.

What if learning to adapt is learning to exist?

We are all part of a humungous space-time continuum, and as creatures, we're merely a blip on the radar. Wouldn't it be helpful to have that perspective more often? Why do we get so disconnected from who we are? Why do we get so attached to meaningless things, whether tangible or virtual? Once we choose to get curious about this, we can expand and experience life to the fullest.

The Dalai Lama XIV said, "People were created to be loved. Things were created to be used. The reason why the world is in chaos is because things are being loved and people are being used."

Instead of staying connected only to the past, to what we have done, we can look for what is not yet created. We could be exploring, questioning, connecting, observing,

_How do we embrace uncertainty and trust that something fascinating will happen as we move forward?_

noticing, being. We could be imagining our spaces as clean slates upon which to draw something new. This goes for what we do personally and professionally; that is, how we spend our time as individuals, with our loved ones, our hobbies, and our communities, and how we spend our time practicing our vocations, whatever they might be.

How can we experience meaningful change, forward momentum, transformation? How can we learn from the snake who sheds its skin? A healthy snake, with access to good nutrition and a balanced ecosystem, will shed its skin on a regular basis—around once a month. This process, called ecdysis, is how snakes grow. Same goes for lobsters. As they grow, they need to shed their rigid exoskeletons and go through a period of significant vulnerability while the new shell sets in place and hardens. Then they live comfortably in the new shell until they outgrow that and go through ecdysis once more. I find this so symbolic of how we, as humans, go through change and adaption: we live, learn, fail, go through discomfort and vulnerability, and reestablish a new sense of self; we grow into ourselves. And some basic human needs—nutrition, rest, social connection, love, self-agency—are necessary for the regular regrowth to occur.

How do we embrace uncertainty and trust that something fascinating will happen as we move forward? Whether it is exhilaration or silence, it might be exactly what we need. How do we learn to adapt, to step into and through the discomfort in order to move into newness? A baby falls down a lot while learning to walk, but she must lean into the discomfort to get to that new level of mobility and freedom.

How will you lead? How will you contribute? How will you live with intention and responsibility and accountability? How and when are you carving out the time and space to reflect on what new world you will create for yourself and for those around you? How will you slow down when you need to? How will you practice patience and allow the path forward to reveal itself?

Performance and forward momentum aren't just about checking items off a list—they're about the big picture, and whether or not you're hitting your long-term, big picture goals. I see my own life as a series of seemingly disparate roles, communities, goals, and identities that all combine together—a collision point of imagination and career and experience. Like one of those amazing recipes where you look at the ingredients list and think, "That stuff won't taste good together," but it does!

As Deepak Chopra wrote in *The Path to Love*, "Uncertainty is your path to freedom." When I first read that line, I thought, "What? No way. I love certainty. I need certainty to feel calm and centered and in control" (i.e., safe). But then I considered it. As an artist, I must embrace uncertainty in the creative process. When you start a thing, you have no idea how it will evolve, what iterations it may or may not go through on its journey to completion—and even completion is uncertain!

It is a conundrum for many of us. We love the familiar. We feel safe. We feel in control. We can go through life on autopilot, so it's easier. But as a popular inspirational quote says, "Ships are safe in the harbor, but that's not what ships were built for."

From the minute we're born, we participate in radical uncertainty. We think we know what's happening. We think we know what will happen because we plan for it. Look at our calendars! Look at our five-year strategic plans! Look at our time management tools! All filled to the brim with certitude, mapped out with surgical precision and ego-controlled, culturally mandated content, created by and for us. And yet, ultimately, it's all a crapshoot. I mean, it's cool when things work out as planned, and you've paid off the house, or written a book, or traversed a continent. That takes thoughtful planning and sacrifice and focused effort. True. A lot of other stuff just happens, or it doesn't.

Some of the most impactful and profound experiences of my life occurred because I embraced uncertainty and got curious. In fact, while in La Jolla, California, at a business conference, I followed my curiosity and ended up meditating with the aforementioned Deepak at his wellness center. Totally random set of circumstances, all leading to something awesome. I'll tell you more about that later, but the main thing is this: there was a decision at hand and I said yes.

And that is what this book is about: embracing uncertainty and getting curious. Leveraging curiosity.

Cultivating curiosity. Releasing judgment and noticing with curiosity.

Curiosity makes us present.

No one can make a perfect road map for personal growth. In fact, it is imperative that when you design your own road map, you take perfection out of the equation. I encourage you to take what you like from this book, leave what you don't. I consider these writings my virtual shoebox. Chances are when you're looking for inspiration in your life, you pull from your own memories and experiences. My hope is that sharing my stories will spark interesting reflections of your own. Included in each section are exercises and challenges, so I encourage you to record your own observations and reflections in whatever mode suits you best (paper notebook, digital tool, voice memo, cave drawings, etc.). Maybe some of you are already thinking, "Who does she think she is? I'm not doing reflection exercises—I hate that stuff!" All good! This is an à la carte menu. Your notes (mental or documented) are of you, by you, and for you only.

Words have incredible power. We can drastically change someone's perspective—including our own—by how we choose to talk about and frame something. (Remember the book from the '80s called *What to Say When You Talk to Yourself*? Same idea.) How can you reframe your life experience in a way that optimizes your ability to move forward with as little friction as possible? In a way that amplifies the positive impact you can have on others? I

wrote this book to experience this process, to reflect on my life through a lens of curiosity and growth, to put it in words on the page, and to then share with others who hopefully continue the conversation. I found this whole book-writing journey fascinating.

I have always been insatiably curious, and because my nickname is Cat, I often think to myself, "Curiosity skilled the Cat." It's how I roll.

It's the main reason I love to read voraciously and pick up new skills. I'm just curious to see what it's all about. Some I practice for a while, some forever, some I try on and discard quickly. But curiosity has led to all of my learning, growth, experience, and meaning. Being willing to take risks is part of what has helped me in my career and other goal-oriented accomplishments.

As my mother regularly tells it, one of my first words was *why*.

And it continues to this day, sometimes to the exasperation of others. I can't help but wonder why. It's like a hunger that I can't fill, or an itch that must be scratched. I just want to know why. Even if I can't understand it, I want to at least *try* to understand it. It's this deep sense of genuine curiosity that has propelled me forward. I'm fascinated by life and life experiences, by the perspectives of others.

Ask my sister, and I'm sure she would tell you it's a pain in the ass to have someone always asking why. Ask my previous romantic partners and they would likely tell you it's a pain in the ass to have someone always asking why. Ask my previous superiors and they would likely tell you it's a pain in the ass to have someone always asking why. But asking why is how we learn important things and move forward, how we tackle stagnancy and trigger creative solutions.

The objective here is to talk about serious things but not take ourselves too seriously. Because curiosity, in and of itself, should be a progressive and positive experience. Even if we're thinking about serious things, even traumatic things, cultivating curiosity is a positive, forward-thinking, progressive, and growth-focused endeavor. Like most of us, I practice life using both wisdom and intuition.

Being open-minded, present, self-aware, and curious helps us understand ourselves, each other, and the world around us a little bit better. Every interaction is an opportunity to gather more insight. Every experience is an opportunity to learn through reflecting, connecting the dots, challenging ourselves, noticing our habits and behaviors and patterns and triggers.

We all want to know where we've come from and where we're going, what we've tried, where we've succeeded, and how we've been challenged. We want to know how to interpret our histories and our present, what we imagine for the future, and the ways we define value. What keeps us up at night? What gets us excited in the morning?

All of these characteristics and practices serve us in our relationships with others and in how we lead. We all play leadership roles—in families, communities, teams, organizations. One of the essential traits of good leadership is clarity. Clarity and curiosity can be a powerful combination, enabling us to get to where we're going even if it's not yet completely defined. We can choose language that is positive, progressive, and outcome-oriented. That is, we might have a clear purpose and goal, but we're open to how we get there, and even open to the possibility of a change in destination.

Ultimately, I hope you find this collection of words and stories and invitations meaningful, inspiring, provocative, and enjoyable.

 **REFLECTIONS**

Where has curiosity served you well?

Where has uncertainty served you well?

*"Come to the edge," he said.*
*"We can't, we're afraid!" they responded.*
*"Come to the edge," he said.*
*"We can't, we will fall!" they responded.*
*"Come to the edge," he said.*
*And so they came.*
*And he pushed them.*
*And they flew.*

GUILLAUME APOLLINAIRE

Talk about moving past fear and choosing yes.

Imagine if they had asked, "Why would you like us to come to the edge?"

They might have flown sooner.

Asking why and exploring, digging deeper, going beyond the surface, with yourself and others, accelerates growth and enables a life well lived.

# Not Knowing the Outcome and Going for It Anyway

*"Be the best. No negativity.
No weakness. No acquiescence to fear
or disaster. No errors of ignorance.
No evasion to reality."*

JEFF BUCKLEY

ONE DAY, AROUND the turn of the twenty-first century, I was at the Rivoli, a bar on Queen Street West in Toronto known for its live music. I was going in to finally talk to the booking agent about doing a few gigs there, of my own music. I had been a songwriter for decades, a light and infrequent performer, and it was time to get my act together and book some real gigs.

Interestingly, although my conversation with the booking agent (Kathryn Gilby) started on that topic, it quickly morphed into something quite different. We discovered we had a mutual love of Jeff Buckley. This was not a common common ground... Not a lot of people that I've talked to in the course of my life even know who he was, never mind his work and the story of his untimely and tragic death. (If you haven't listened to his album *Grace*, do it. Listen to it at least three times. It is so unique and so musically rich and layered, you need to get your soul around it. Call me when you're done.) Anyway, during the conversation, I shared that I had heard about venues in New York and

*I walked outside and thought, "What the hell have I just committed to?"*

Chicago putting on multi-artist tribute shows and how great it would be if someone did that in Toronto.

She said to me, "Let's do it." I said, "Huh?" and she said, "Let's do it. You produce it, you host it. We'll gather musicians together, promote it together, it'll be great."

I said, "Uh, yeah, sure."

I walked outside and thought, "What the hell have I just committed to? I don't know how to produce a tribute show!" I wanted to turn around and say, "You got the wrong gal." But I didn't. I stayed curious: What might this be like? What could I learn? Who could I call to help me? What's the worst thing that could happen—it's a flop and no one comes? Could I live with that? Yup. So, let's go for it. And that's what we did. And I learned as I went along.

First, I decided to stay true to my values, which specifically meant don't take advantage of this person's image/music/etc. I wanted to do this tribute respectfully. So, I looked up the phone number for the Jeff Buckley estate in New York City and gave them a call. Told them the situation and that we wanted their blessing, and that all the proceeds would go to charity. They were thrilled. And guess what happened next?

They put me on the phone with Jeff's mom, Mary. We became lifelong friends. They connected me with the folks in Chicago who were doing the tribute there, Michael and Helen . . . and they became my friends. I went to Chicago to play in their annual tribute—and made more friends from around the world. We invited all those performers to play the upcoming Toronto shows. Many of them did!

We ended up having three nights of shows because so many performers wanted to be part of it. We received donations of gear, promotion, beer. All the musicians donated their time and talent. We raised more than $5,000 for Regent Park School of Music (Toronto) and Road Recovery (NYC). I made lifelong friends, and over the next many years, I met interesting people and had interesting experiences thanks to those friendships. Like having dinner with songwriter J.D. Souther (Eagles, Linda Ronstadt) because he was in town on tour with my friend and fellow Buckley tribute player April Smith.

I learned how to produce and host a show. I played a lot of live shows. I met Mike Borkosky who would help me make my first record. And our production team went on to produce five more tribute shows over the next ten years ... resulting in more than $20,000 raised for charity.

All because I chose to stay curious (and fight the fear!) and be okay with uncertainty.

And check this out: my dear friend Andy Ackland, who had invited me to see Jeff Buckley play at the Starfish Room in Vancouver in 1994, ended up recording Jeff's mom playing cello for a song on my album *Twelve* in 2004. Full circle.

Here's a track from *Twelve* where I allude to *Grace*.

**"All I Need Is You"**

Hundred miles for your smile when I walk in the door
Take my hand, understand that we've been here before
Pour a drink, let me think about this crazy world
we're living in
When I see you, there is one thing I cannot deny

All I need is you to get me through the day
All I need is you to make me feel okay

Lost and found, losing ground, we were already dead
All the drinking led to thinking it was all in my head
See your face, think of *Grace*, brings me back
to that easy time
When I see you, there is something I cannot deny

All I need is you to get me through the day
All I need is you to make me feel okay

And don't you worry, babe, it's okay, we can figure it out
We'll find another way

 catherineharrison.com

# A Series of
# Yesses

*"I think we should go ahead with the show even if I had to sit out there on the front porch with a guitar by myself."*

JACK WHITE

PLAYING THE BUCKLEY tribute show in Chicago led to me meeting and befriending an Italian musician named Claudia. A few years later, Claudia started dating a drummer named Matt Johnson. Matt Johnson used to play with Jeff Buckley. As it happened, in June 2008, Claudia was coming to New York City to spend a week with Matt. I was invited to travel down from Toronto and stay with them for a long weekend. Our plans were solidified in April.

As life and death would have it, my dad died just three weeks before the planned trip. The sudden loss of my dad was devastating to me, and the ensuing weeks were emotionally, mentally, and physically exhausting. I considered not going to NYC but decided I needed to get away, and that my dad would have been the first to recommend it.

At the time, Matt was playing with Martha Wainwright. (He's played with both Rufus and Martha over the years.) The last night of my visit, Claudia and I went to his gig at Joe's Pub. This cabaret theater, situated right between

Greenwich Village and Alphabet City, is ranked by *Rolling Stone* as one of the best live venues in the US and it's where Amy Winehouse and Adele made their North American debuts. It is a beautiful space and has incredible sound and ambiance. Near the end of the show, Martha's mother, Kate McGarrigle, joined her for a few intimate mother/daughter tunes. This parent/child bonding moment did me in. My dad and I had always bonded over music. Being steeped in that musical environment, watching and listening to moving vocal harmonies was a profound experience in my early grieving period. At the trendy after-show party, Kate was kind and sensitive and comforted me in my grief

*The day of the show, I bought a single ticket—"Give me the best one you got!"—and headed downtown.*

over the loss of my father. As it happens, she died only eighteen months later.

Fast-forward two years and Rufus Wainwright was playing the Elgin Theatre as part of the Luminato Festival in Toronto. I had always loved Rufus's work. The day of the show, I bought a single ticket—"Give me the best one you got!"—and headed downtown. Before the show began, I chatted with the tour manager at the merchandise table. I asked if Matt was playing the gig. No, this was a solo Rufus gig, just him and a piano.

In chatting with the tour manager, David, I shared my story of Kate being so kind to me after my dad died, and that I'd love to tell Rufus that story about his mom, as he had lost her just months earlier. David thought that was a great idea and invited me to the backstage party. After the fantastic show, I headed to the elevators to go the party, but first had to pass security. Key learning—even with an invitation, one must be very persistent to get through the myriad checkpoints to get backstage at the Elgin Theatre. However, all of a sudden, there I was, and there he was, and I was able to tell Rufus the story myself.

He then invited me to stay for the party and I met tons of interesting and wonderful people from around the world. Sound and lighting people from Sweden and Italy, sound techs from Australia, and a bunch of lovely US and Canadian folks too. And that is how a little series of yesses can lead to magical experiences.

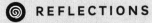

## ◎ REFLECTIONS

Reflect on an experience where you committed to doing something without all the answers. (You may have even felt scared to do it!)

How did curiosity play a part?

Who did you meet?

What did you learn?

How did it change the course of your life?

How can you leverage this knowledge of self, and your own experience, to cultivate curiosity in your present life?

Where would you like to be more curious?

# Originality

ask
believe
receive

USED TO GET stressed out about whether my songs were "original" enough. Or I'd get stressed when some one heard one of my songs and said, "Oh, that's great, but it sounds just like X." To me it was some sort of judgment and limitation on the value of that song. I would question myself: Did I copy it? Am I an unwitting plagiarist? Am I a fraud? In those times, I reminded myself that I am but a blip of a human in the vast construct of time and space. Certain outputs will resemble my predecessors' outputs. There are only three colors. There are only twelve notes. These are the fundamentals. Certain things go well together and it's mathematically likely there will be similarities.

Beethoven, Beach Boys, Beyoncé—all their songs are made up of the same notes. Paintings hanging in the AGO or the MOMA, kindergarten finger paintings, street graffiti—all made up of the same colors. Take a five-minute break and Google "forty songs with the same chords" and you'll find lots of popular songs with the same chords, the same structure. For instance, you might never think about how much in common the Beatles' "Let It Be," Adele's "Someone Like You," and Journey's "Don't Stop Believin'" have in common. They are hook-y because they are familiar to us. In my line of professional work, we business consultants all use pretty much the same content over and over—good selling skills and leadership skills and active listening and performance and behavior change—and we continue to boil down to the same stuff we've been talking about for decades.

There is no originality. What we think of as originality is merely the fearless authentic expression of what we see, hear, feel, absorb, and experience through the lens of our own personal journey. That is, creativity is the synthesis of myriad data points being mixed in infinite ways, and originality is putting all of those data points and confabulations through the lens of an individual's unique life experience. (Again, this is just my take on it . . . get curious about your own take on it!)

Consider collective consciousness and how people create similar things at the same time. It is unrealistic (in fact, quite egocentric) to think that you would sit in your little space of the world, one of more than seven billion people, and create something completely original out of thin air.

Here's a funny story that illustrates this posit.

While hiking with a friend one day, we were lamenting the random, yet frequent, run-ins with individuals who, to be frank, behave like dicks. I said, "I'm going to write a

*There are only three colors. There are only twelve notes. These are the fundamentals. Certain things go well together and it's mathematically likely there will be similarities.*

book called *Don't Be a Dick: A How-to Guide*. It would be a tongue-in-cheek little tome, a simple, easy, step-by-step approach to getting more of what you want in life and less of what you don't." And we laughed and laughed. And, of course, I thought, "Oh, I'm going to do it! Just for fun!"

As this little project was not a priority for me at the time, it bubbled away on the back burner of my creative stove for a few months. I kept chuckling at the notion of it. And then one day, I was reading a *Psychology Today* at my local library (I love libraries!). Near the end of the publication, I saw an ad for a book titled *Don't Be a Dick* by Mark B. Borg Jr. (2019). It was literally being published at the same time I had the idea. Seriously!!!

And *that* is universal consciousness at play.

So, don't get too judge-y on yourself when it comes to being original. Just be you. Don't block yourself. Be willing to give yourself permission to investigate. You don't need to commit to anything; you just need to investigate, be curious. Just do it. Put it out there.

I coined the phrase "verbal acupuncture" to introduce myself at speaking engagements. What the heck does that mean?

It means that I probably don't say anything or convey anything or create anything that you don't already know or that doesn't already exist. It means I gather and select content and ideas that I find really interesting and fascinating and that investigates how humans work together, live together, progress together, and try to connect together in meaningful ways. It means that when I say something, I'm like an acupuncture needle: I'm triggering something in you that already exists. I'm triggering knowledge that already resides within you and stimulating that meridian to make you go, "Oh yeah, I know that," or "I used to know that," "I used to do that," or "I know that, but I don't do it," or "Hmmm..."

Verbal acupuncture is using words and ideas to hopefully reenergize and reconnect parts of you that are possibly lying dormant or blocked. To stimulate your curiosity about what's going on in your life and what resources, knowledge, and know-how you already have in order to leverage the good and remediate the less-than-good.

The reality is if I'm thinking something, probably millions of others are too, or have over millennia thought about it, and created something with it somewhere. Just like the concept I explored earlier of three colors, twelve notes.

Sometimes it's simply those who get curious and ask the most questions, the right questions, and follow the thread further, who truly innovate and change the world.

## ⊚ REFLECTIONS

When has something like the *Don't Be a Dick* story happened in your life?

Where are you holding yourself back because you think you're not original enough?

What do you know but don't do?

What knowledge would you like to reconnect to?

How would you like to activate your inner knowledge to realize more health and well-being?

# Beautiful
# Tornado

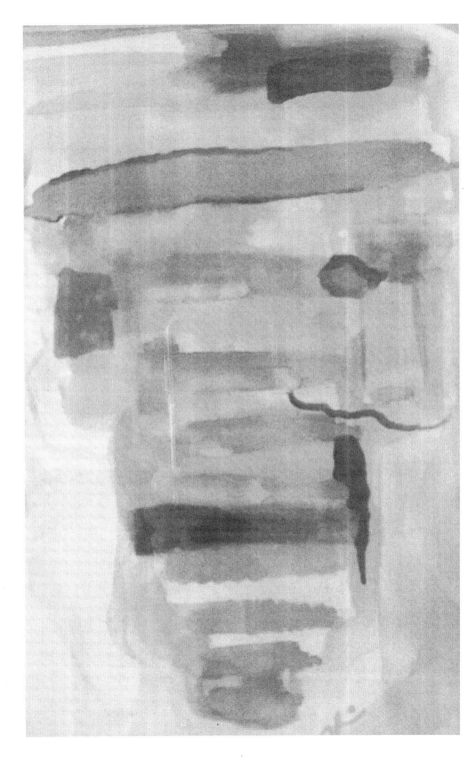

I PAINTED THIS WATERCOLOR painting while living in Vancouver. It was an abstract, but the image that emerged looked like a blend of Africa and a face, and it started to represent to me the multicolored, multifaceted world we all live in and which lives within each of us.

Upon seeing this painting, one of my young nieces exclaimed, "Oh, what a beautiful tornado!"

That's where curiosity and creativity and uncertainty take you on a journey. I loved that phrase. So, I wrote a song entitled "Beautiful Tornado." Here are the lyrics:

Head keeps spinning, lost my footing, I'm feeling low
They keep winning, or so it seems, and I'm in slo-mo
I go crazy in the moonlight, it's the curse of my sign
There's no answer when you call me, I'm just doing
my time

But I love you so completely, like red roses and wine
You're the one thing I can count on, so please don't
pay me no mind

Hit the highway, on a road trip, to escape this disguise
At a truck stop, I grab a coffee to rebuild my mind
Send me flowers on a black day and you can kiss me
goodbye
'Cause I'm an airplane in a spiral, alone in the sky

I take comfort, in the darkness, where I hide my tears
Yet you linger, and kiss my fingers, to kill off those fears
In the moonlight, in the starlight, on an indigo shell
You see through it, past the bullshit, who could know
me so well?

In this beautiful tornado, I go 'round and 'round
In this beautiful tornado, you pull me back down

 catherineharrison.com

# Getting a Job,
# Building a Career

*"It's your attitude, not your aptitude, that determines your altitude."*

ZIG ZIGLAR
(AND MY MOM, REPEATEDLY—
JUST ASK THE GRANDKIDS)

I FELL INTO MY career. Right time, right place, right contacts. (I really had no "When I grow up, I want to be..." plans.)

In 1986, while at the University of Western Ontario, I got a summer job at a pharmaceutical company near home. I worked in microbiology and chemistry labs for three summers. Although I never would've considered doing this work, I found it fascinating to see what happens in a pharmaceutical manufacturing facility. In the labs, we had to run all the quality-control processes to ensure quality and safety standards were met, and then follow the manufacturing process from raw materials to final product, and even beyond. Stability testing enabled us to know how long a drug was effective (basically validating the expiry date and calculating efficacy beyond six, twelve, eighteen, twenty-four months).

We cooked the agar. We filled the petri dishes. We swabbed anything and everything in the facility and made cultures to ensure cleanliness and adherence to the

---

*Upon reflection, the only professional regrets I have are connected to times when I was scared. When I let fear lead, instead of curiosity.*

---

parameters of safety, quality, and effectiveness. We tested the medicines at every level of production and storage to ensure it was what we thought it was, to validate quality. Fascinating stuff.

In 1989, I graduated, got a pharmaceutical sales rep job in Toronto, and thus started my twenty-two-year career in the pharmaceutical industry. For me, it was the perfect blend of science, business, lots of young smart fun people, great money ($27K!) with a company car (Chevrolet Lumina!), benefits, and bonuses. The sky was the limit and the world was my oyster.

---

*WHOA! Important backstory here*

When I graduated from university, I had no intention of getting a job. I wanted to travel the world, play guitar, meet people, see places, learn languages, be free and easy. As I was planning to go to Europe with my boyfriend for the standard post-university backpacking trip, it became apparent that one needed money to do such a thing.

I needed a job. A good job. So, after much deliberation, I went to an interview for the pharma sales rep gig at the same company where I'd worked my summers, got the job, and made a pact with myself that after two years, I would quit and go traveling.

*That story later—did she? Didn't she? Stay tuned . . .*

---

You might ask, "How does curiosity fit into the world of work?" I respond, "How can it not?"

All innovation, creativity, brainstorming, et cetera requires a sense of curiosity to begin and continue. I will say that almost all of my professional endeavors have happened because of my innate curiosity. If I didn't try it, how would I know? Upon reflection, the only professional regrets I have are connected to times when I was scared. When I let fear lead, instead of curiosity. There are certain roles that I did not accept, that I did not even attempt to take on, because I was afraid of failure. Or of making the wrong choice. Having to commit to a choice, which felt like I would then lose the option of ongoing choice. Instead of recognizing that in every moment I have a choice—to continue, to stop, to learn, to reflect.

---

*Okay, here's what happened*

I worked for two years and two months. Planned my escape. Everyone (e-v-e-r-y-o-n-e!) told me to keep this lucrative, professional job: "Everyone is trying to get into this industry and you're going to quit!?!? You're only twenty-six. What are you thinking?"

---

Well, what I was thinking was this:

*If I don't go now, I won't ever go. Likely,
life will take on more momentum and greater
responsibilities, and twists and turns that may prevent
me from having this chance to travel unencumbered.
I now have two years' experience, a pretty good résumé,
good contacts in the industry, a bunch of money in the
bank (savings plus the travel money), and, worst case, I come
home and paint houses for a living until I get another great job.*

*If I did it once, I can do it again.
I'm curious about the world and my place in it!
I want to know how I will handle the stresses
and uncertainties of traveling (mostly alone).*

*I have to do this.*

*"Live with no excuses and travel with no regrets."*

OSCAR WILDE

# Travel

I've always been a true Gemini when it comes to planning. On the one hand, I want to know exactly what's going on so I can relax (and have some say in my experience). On the other hand, I hate planning, as I want to just be in the moment and do whatever I want, when I want, and roll with what happens.

Traveling is the perfect opportunity to leverage both of those positions and, interestingly, not always when you want to employ one versus the other.

---

At the time I quit my job, I was dating a guy who lived out west. He had recently moved from Edmonton to Vancouver. I was getting rid of my apartment in Toronto to travel. Why not move to Vancouver too? I was curious! So, in July 1992, I packed a moving crate, got on a plane, and moved to Vancouver. *More on that later.*

---

In early September, I set off to Europe, India, and Nepal. The first two weeks, I traveled with my mom. She was finishing her EdD and had been working her butt off. We'd decided to do a little mom/daughter jaunt through Europe. I advised her, candidly, that this would be the two- or three-star version of traveling, not the style of vacationing to which she was accustomed. (She managed this reality by booking a five-star Mediterranean cruise at the end of our two weeks together to recover and get back her balance. Smart lady.)

## What Did I Learn While on the Backpacking Trip?

I learned even the best laid plans go awry. I learned that when I have no one to rely on, I'm pretty self-sufficient. I learned I can deal with a lot of adversity if I just stay calm and trust my intuition. I learned that money helps (backpacking with an AMEX gold card as a backup comes in handy—another bonus of having two years' worth of disciplined savings in the bank). I learned people are the same everywhere—learn to say the basics in every language you can and you'll have instant human connection.

I learned you can do a lot of laundry in the shower or bath. I learned I love sleep—and I take my napping seriously. I learned I can live for three months with a very limited amount of clothing, toiletries, and belongings, so I could likely do that forever. I learned you must wash your hands. You can get violently ill in the Himalayan foothills if you accept an orange from a goatherd and eat it. The rule was "only eat what you can peel." So, I did. But I ate with the hands that peeled it.

I learned there is beauty everywhere. I learned sometimes you can do reckless things and live to tell the tale. I learned sometimes you can't.

I learned that the night sky in snowy mountains is an experience worth getting up for. Every single night. Even when you're sleeping in a freezing cold tent with all your belongings on. I learned sunrises are worth getting up for. (See note re: how much I love sleep. Recognize the depth of this sacrifice—still worth it!)

I learned to appreciate disconnecting from distractions. I learned to appreciate a letter sent across the world. I learned to appreciate a phone call. (This was pre-internet, pre–cell phone.) I learned loneliness is an inside job. You can be alone and love it or be alone and hate it. I learned I like being alone. I learned I like being with others. I like

---

*Trust your gut and
speak your truth.*

---

meeting new people. I like missing those I love. I like reconnecting with those I love.

I learned that Curiosity + Trusting Your Gut = Great Experiences.

I learned intuition and claiming personal power might prevent bad things from happening. To this day, I am certain that by trusting my gut I avoided being taken to the outskirts of New Delhi to be who-knows-what by my rickshaw driver or other ne'er-do-wells. We had been doing a "tour" for hours. Mostly in central New Delhi. Lots of people. All good. Suddenly, we were on a quiet road heading out of town. I had a bad feeling.

ME: "Hey, where are we going?
HIM: "Tourist place!"
ME: "I don't think so. I'd like to turn back."
HIM: "Very nice, yes, we go there."
ME: "Turn this f$%^#!@ thing around right now or
    I will lose my s%&^ on you!!"
HIM: "Okay."

That was a go/no-go situation. I learned you must trust your gut and speak your truth. Fast and forthright.

## From Prague to Whitehorse

Here's a great example of being curious and open-ended.

My friend, Greg, and I met up in Prague at the time of Major League Baseball's '92 World Series finals. The Toronto Blue Jays were playing the Atlanta Braves. We really wanted to be able to watch the game (remember this is pre–global connectivity). Not a lot of places we went to even had a TV, never mind satellite, never mind sports satellite. We wandered into a little family run bar, and lo and behold on the TV was a soccer match. Boom. Opportunity. We asked to speak with the owner/manager. We ordered some drinks and told him our plight. That our home team was facing off against "the Americans" in the final. Was there any way he could let us watch the game (starting at one a.m. Prague time) here at his pub while it was closed? He said as long as we brought our own food and beer and remembered to lock up, yes. So, we went shopping for game supplies, went to our hostel for a rest, and came back to the closed empty bar at 12:30 a.m. to watch the epic 1992 Blue Jays World Series win (the overtime game continued until 6:11 a.m. Prague time).

If we hadn't been curious as to how, when, or where the opportunity might materialize, we likely would've assumed that watching the game was impossible, and it would have been. And think about the uncertainty the bar owner chose to accept by letting two strangers have access to his property in the middle of the night! Tremendous.

Whitehorse, 26 July

Hi Catherine,

I'm finally getting around to sending you these photos — sorry I took so long.

If you're coming back up here, I hope you'll be in touch.

I'm having a good summer, hope you are too.

Julie

Here's another one.

When I was working as a sales rep in Vancouver, part of my territory was Whitehorse, Yukon. I made my sales calls by telephone, and then I sent samples, product information, and patient support materials by mail. The plan was to fly up once or twice a year.

My first trip, I was excited. I was going to Whitehorse! I booked my flight, booked a few meetings with key customers and a hotel room, and off I went. Absolutely beautiful flight... nothing but gorgeous wilderness and then mountains, mountains, mountains.

I spent two days doing my job, albeit relatively unsuccessfully. I had assumed that customers would be thrilled to see a rep who flew all the way in from the city, but as it turned out, they weren't. It was actually a pretty hostile little medical community toward new reps. The old-timer reps were all best buddies who partied with the doctors, but for newbies like me, it was a non-starter. Nonetheless, I did my best and then headed to the airport to go back to Vancouver.

Two things happened: one, the actor Corbin Bernsen was sitting next to me, and I loved *L.A. Law*, so that was cool, and two, they had overbooked the flight and asked if anyone was willing to get off the plane and catch a flight the next day. The reward was a free round-trip flight anywhere in North America. I was from Toronto, and my family still lived there, so going home was always a priority for me. I quickly raised my hand. And off the plane I went, along with a handful of others.

While waiting for our travel vouchers, I started talking with a woman who had also disembarked. She was a local photographer. She was going out that afternoon to take photos in the wilderness. Did I want to come? I didn't have any clothes other than my business stuff. I said sure... can I borrow some clothes and hiking boots? She looked me up and down, determined we were "close enough" in size, and said, "I've got lots of stuff you can wear!"

And that is how I got to go into the Yukon wilderness with a fantastic person to spend a super cool twenty-four hours that I otherwise wouldn't have had. Curiosity and saying yes brought adventure and joy and exploration to my life. And a free round-trip ticket.

 **REFLECTIONS**

Think of a time in your life where something seemingly impossible turned out to be quite awesome simply because you kept an open, curious mind and released the attachment to the specifics of "How?"

Where might you use that approach in your current life?

What do you need to do next?

# Reentry Points and Finding Adventure

*"Creativity is about choosing curiosity over fear."*

ELIZABETH GILBERT

AFTER TRAVELING AROUND the world, I experienced serious reassimilation challenges upon returning to my middle-class realities. I had spent a month in Nepal, surrounded by people who live in villages on dollars a month. When I returned to my family and my fancy Canadian lifestyle (Toronto, Whistler, Vancouver) in '93, I think I was a bit of—a lot of?—a pain in the ass to anyone who had stuff or worked hard for stuff. Perspective is one of the greatest gifts of traveling, seeing how other people live, struggle, celebrate, connect, and find purpose and meaning in their days. I saw our extremely fortunate life back home in Canada through an entirely new lens, and the rampant consumerism that is Western culture was not only tough to reintegrate into, but I found it abhorrent. To a large extent, I still do.

I leveraged my curiosity to travel the West Coast a bit. I chose to go to California to hang out with some people I'd met in Europe. Hung out in Baja, Mexico, with the locals. Used up all my remaining money. (And much love to the boyfriend who paid the rent while all this self-discovery was going on!)

Later in '93, it was time to get a job. Did I go back to pharmaceutical sales? Absolutely not! Couldn't do it. Needed to transition. Got a waitressing job at The Keg on Granville Island, Vancouver. Waiting tables in a busy tourist area is a great way to learn more about human behavior, my own and others'. I met some new people—my peers—and partied with a few of them but didn't make any real connections. I felt like an outsider. I chose to use that job purely as a transactional opportunity to make some cash. Alongside that work, I decided to leverage my university education and got certified as a personal trainer and nutritional coach. I set up my own personal wellness consulting company and dabbled with different approaches to finding clients (partnering with local gyms and health products, making paper flyers and displaying them in doctors' offices). Although I was passionate about health and wellness, I wasn't passionate about selling my services to others. It fizzled out after six months. After that, I worked as a receptionist at the Vancouver Art Gallery for a few months. I was trained as a Starbucks barista just to see what this new company was all about. I never worked in a store, but I enjoyed learning about the inner workings of the organization. I probably did other short-term gigs that I just can't recall.

Again, I was lucky that I had a boyfriend who was working full-time and paying our main living expenses. And

*All of these learning experiences began with CURIOSITY!*

I didn't have a very expensive lifestyle (except skiing). I took full advantage of the fact that I was living in one of the most beautiful places on Earth with a guy who was full of life and adventure. I will always be grateful to him for introducing me to a vast array of outdoor adventures. I learned to sail. I learned to hang-glide/paraglide. I learned to sea kayak. I learned to rock climb. I skied Whistler, the Okanagan, and the Rockies. I enjoyed 300 kilometer cycling/camping trips through Alberta and BC. I learned to love the rain. He was the one who had done all these things before. For me, it was all new, kind of scary, and very exciting. All of these learning experiences began with CURIOSITY!

## Painting 101

Picture this: a gorgeous spring day in Stanley Park, Vancouver. My boyfriend and I were walking through an outdoor art show. I notice a big, colorful, abstract painting of a dog. I wanted it for the apartment. It was $450. I said, "$450! I could paint that myself!"

So, the next day, I went to the local art store; bought a canvas, a bunch of paint, some brushes, a color wheel; and starting painting.

My first paintings were atrocious (it turns out, I could not "paint that myself"). They would have fit well on the walls of an elementary school. Parents would have been proud of their seven-year-old's work. I still have a few of them, some have been adjusted over the years, but some remain as is—a good reminder of where I started. Many of my other first editions were painted over... No sense wasting good canvas.

I loved the whole process. I stretched and primed my own canvas, built my own frames. I loved hanging out at the art store on Granville Island, reveling in the possibility of materials, approaches, styles. Mostly I loved the *uncertainty* of how it would turn out. *Uncertainty is your path to freedom.*

I took a watercolor course at Emily Carr University of Art + Design. The course was interesting, but watercolor painting was not for me. I bought a metal folding-tray palette kit of watercolor paints and began taking it everywhere. I tried to be that artist who paints in parks and on beaches. I did it for a while, but it didn't stick. I took a sketching course. Good for perspective and planning paintings, but realism was not for me.

Over the years, I have refined my style to be my own. Colorful, dynamic, flowing. Often with words or symbols. Integrated communication of something I want to say. To connect to another. These are also the pieces that most resonate with others.

Authentic representation of yourself connects you with others. To this day, what drives me to a museum or an art gallery is curiosity. I want to see how others interpret the world, their thoughts and feelings, through art. I'm curious to see how others use various media to make the art take on the personality of the artist, the cause, the muse, or whatever. Even if I don't like the art (which is subjective), I respect the process, the engagement, the commitment of doing it, and putting it out there.

CURIOSITY = Engagement, Interest, Growth
Seek and Ye Shall Find!
(Or not... but if you keep your eyes, ears, mind, and heart open, you will learn something along the way.)

My favorite reflections at the end of the day include me thinking, "Hm. That was interesting!" Whether it was good, bad, or neutral, if I learn something about myself or the world around me, I can see it as enlightening.

## Be Curious Now!

How would you draw a flower, a dog, a mountain, a tree?
Draw your versions here. Now. No need to fret. No one is
watching. (Aren't you curious??)

   Remember when you were a kid? You used to draw stuff
all the time. You were curious to see what it would look
like on the page. You might even have been curious about
how to communicate what you saw in your mind and how
you wanted it represented on the page. Just do it. See what
happens. It's okay.

| Flower | Dog |
|---|---|
| | |
| **Mountain** | **Tree** |
| | |

## ⊚ REFLECTIONS

What is one thing you would like to know more about today? (It might be as simple as "Where do capers come from?" I learned about that yesterday!)

If you were given two hours today to learn anything at all, what might it be?

Challenge yourself to identify at least one thing you learned today—it might be knowledge, you might have had a new experience, it might be wisdom based on a success or a mistake.

If you can't find one thing from today, plan one thing for tomorrow.

# That Self-Talk Bubble

*"Where there is an emptiness, the mind will obligingly fill it up. Fear is always at hand to supply any vacancies, as is curiosity. I have had ample experience with both."*

MARGARET ATWOOD,
*THE TESTAMENTS*

CURIOSITY IS OFTEN thwarted by a heavy rotation of self-limiting thoughts.

We all have one: a cartoon-like bubble above our heads filled with thoughts, beliefs, judgments, assumptions, fears, biases, and experiences that colors our ability to truly be present and engaged in an exchange with another human being (who, by the way, also has their own bubble).

Often the chatter is so loud, we cannot attend to what is actually happening. For example, when we know we need to contribute to a group brainstorming session, when we are participating in a meeting, when we are on a first date, when we are embroiled in an argument with a loved one, when we are in an interview (hiring or applying) or performance review, our thoughts can distract from the matter at hand. Sound familiar?

The ability to manage this bubble is a critical success factor for cultivating presence and creating the conditions for effective connection and communication with others. But before we can manage it, we have to know: why do we have that bubble, anyway? It's created over a lifetime of experiences and observations and from listening to and consuming the information and opinions of others—usually influential others.

It starts with our families of origin and spirals outward, as we become more independent. We observe and experience the highs and lows of interacting with peers, classmates, friends, strangers, teammates, loved ones, and authority figures. We listen, watch, and absorb an incessant stream of media images, commentary, and directives telling us how to live our lives and, usually, how we are deficient and need X to complete us.

We continually feed the bubble with what we pay attention to. We continue feeding the bubble, instead of managing it, by taking in the same kinds of information, biases, assumptions, and judgments that formed it. Alternatively, we can choose to feed it a new healthier diet that is more open and fluid. We can manage the bubble's control over our ability to be present in a given moment.

The bubble is associated in large part with the amygdala, the oldest part of the brain, dedicated to survival. It is where the fight-flight-or-freeze mechanism lives. Neuroscience has shown that parts of the brain associated with listening actually turn off when the bubble is activated too rigorously. (Read David Rock's *Your Brain at Work* for more on this.)

One powerful example of how our bubble of beliefs can be reinforced is something called confirmation bias—i.e., hearing only what confirms our preexisting beliefs. For example, if we go into an exchange with another person believing that they are difficult, temperamental, or irrational, what we most notice and remember is any behavior that validates our preexisting belief. Our brains ignore or discount behavior that does not align with those beliefs. If we are unaware that we are doing this, we create an inaccurate and self-reinforcing distortion of the world, and of the people around us.

Confirmation bias shows up most clearly in our social media communities. We follow and like that which we already agree with, while ignoring people we disagree with. We end up intensifying our positions and minimizing our appreciation of different perspectives.

So, how do we manage the bubble? It takes awareness and practice.

The first step is to cultivate awareness that the bubble exists, and to acknowledge that we are often listening to the bubble and not the other person in a dialogue. It takes a continual, conscious effort to shift our attention from the bubble to the other person. It means accepting that we all have unconscious biases and protectionism built deep into our human coding. If we don't accept it's there, we certainly can't learn more about it.

Managing the bubble is about quieting our own chatter so as to be present and respectful of the other person. We can tell when someone is not actually listening to us, either while we are talking or as soon as they open their mouths to express their opinion with no regard for what we have just shared. Let us choose to learn to manage the bubble and lead by example.

This can be difficult at first. We want to formulate retorts and counterattacks, to sound smart and competent and in control. Yes, control. When we accept the notion of impermanence and constant change, we must step into the unknown and relinquish control. It doesn't mean giving up thoughtful planning or implementing action steps. It means we recognize the fluidity of any situation and set forth with the knowledge that things will shift along the way. Even in a simple interaction with another human being, accepting what is and managing your own mental chatter reveal a whole host of otherwise missed insights and opportunities to connect.

We need to learn that truly hearing another person, empathizing and engaging in a present manner, is far more powerful and sustainable than shouting our own agenda.

When you feel your bubble getting out of control, think of the acronym CAR:

C – Check yourself.
A – Assess the situation rationally and challenge assumptions.
R – Respond accordingly.

I use this acronym because it is easy to remember and easy to relate to. Imagine you're in traffic and someone

*C* – *Check yourself.*

*A* – *Assess the situation rationally and challenge assumptions.*

*R* – *Respond accordingly.*

cuts you off. You can easily lose yourself in the bubble, assigning character traits to the other driver based on the car model, color, etc. You then start to assign intention too! They did it on purpose to piss you off, they don't like people in your kind of car, etc. Then you react with irrational emotions (often accompanied by gestures and words). Really, you are a captive to the bubble and no one is necessarily affected but you. You can stop the cycle in the moment by becoming more aware of your response, assessing the situation rationally, and moving forward.

For people who struggle to manage their bubbles, I recommend creating the conditions to be present in the moment—turn your phone off (or leave it behind) when you're in a meeting, at a social event, or in conversation. Seek out perspectives that are different from your own, and make a deliberate effort to truly engage with new ideas.

Like any new behavior, learning to manage your bubble will be difficult at first, but with sustained and deliberate effort you can quiet the chatter and cultivate presence. A sense of flow comes to the interaction when we consciously choose to stop listening to the bubble (engaging only with our own thoughts and egos) and attend to what the other is actually saying. In *On Becoming a Person,* Carl Rogers referred to unconditional positive regard as one of the fundamental aspects of successfully dealing with others. In order to do so, you must actually care about what the other person is saying, as is. As Stephen Covey, who wrote *The 7 Habits of Highly Effective People*, said, "Seek first to understand, then be understood."

The good news is that the bubble is dynamic and malleable. We can control it, not be victim to it. It is a choice: to notice, to shift, to practice, and to create more positive and productive ways of engaging with the people around us.

# Mindfulness: Learning and Leading

*"Mindfulness is the aware, balanced acceptance of the present experience. It isn't more complicated than that. It is opening to or receiving the present moment, pleasant or unpleasant, just as it is, without either clinging to it or rejecting it."*

SYLVIA BOORSTEIN

**M**INDFULNESS IS THE ability to observe all that chatter, notice it, manage it. And be fully present to the task at hand, to the conversations at hand, to the decision at hand.

Mindfulness helps steady a leader, particularly when things are chaotic. And a steady leader helps steady others.

A mindful leader learns to accept whatever arises without getting caught in judgmental good/bad thinking. There's no repression of a feeling or thought, but no acting out of it either. There is a comfort with the humanness of ourselves, of our reactions, with the chaos.

As time goes on, as a mindful leader, you develop strength and resilience to be comfortable with the uncomfortable. You can approach uncertainty and volatility with a sense of humor and humility. And the degree to which you can be present and friendly toward yourself is the degree to which you can do so with others.

Mindful leaders are solution-oriented and are able to more effectively navigate the duality of both the right now and the future, exploring possibilities with a curious mind. They can also hold opposing thoughts at the same time, which prevents limited binary thinking. This is so critical for innovative leadership and for leadership during crisis.

Once you name the feeling—anger, sadness, fear, loneliness, tightness in your chest—choosing the next step becomes a conscious choice. A good example is the hamster wheel of rumination many of us are familiar with. It's okay to notice it, accept it, and then say, "Yeah, not feeding that rodent right now! I'm going to put energy elsewhere." Maybe even laugh at it. Get present. Let it go.

The leader who practices mindfulness is then also able to be fully present with others, to cultivate real connectedness—with peers, team members, clients. That alone can help minimize others' stress responses and enable them to open up, to access their creative problem-solving abilities, and to cocreate new paths forward.

They call it a mindfulness practice because you have to do it over and over and over... and cultivate the habit. You begin to notice more, see the patterns, be more present and engaged with yourself and others, and you can lead more effectively through any situation, including an unprecedented global pandemic.

Connecting and communicating with others is at the heart of every human interaction. Managing the bubble and getting present in the moment help you create and sustain more meaningful and productive personal and professional relationships.

*Mindfulness helps steady
a leader, particularly
when things are chaotic.
And a steady leader
helps steady others.*

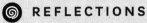

## ◎ REFLECTIONS

Where in your life do you most need to manage your bubble?

What do you notice when you listen to it? What are you saying to yourself?

How can you adjust that self-talk to be more compassionate, curious, present? With yourself? With those around you?

# Motorcycles, Hang-Gliding, and Other Things That Scared My Mother

*"It is not true that people stop pursuing dreams because they grow old; they grow old because they stop pursuing dreams."*

GABRÍEL GARCIA MÁRQUEZ

THROUGHOUT MY LIFE, I have been exposed to experiences through others—friends, boyfriends, colleagues, people I've met on my travels—and my curiosity has led me to explore how and when these activities might enrich my life.

My simple reality is that watching others do things makes me wonder, "What would that be like? How can I just begin?" I do not have, perhaps surprisingly, a reckless attitude or a thrill-seeking character. In fact, I'm pretty safety conscious, and thrill-seeking per se is not my jam. Roller coasters? No thanks. Riding on the back of someone's motorcycle? Don't like it. However, learning a skill myself, even just to a beginner level, is very interesting. It gives me a firsthand perspective that is otherwise out of reach.

Sometimes the skill remains a lifelong passion—skiing mountains, for example. I have also had the thrill of going down a mountain upside down, wrapped in the first-aid toboggan! Yup, garage sale in a back bowl full of

moguls. Blew a knee. (Translation: bad ski accident on a mountain.)

Other times—getting my motorcycle license, buying one, and then having a motorcycle accident because a Ford F-250 didn't see me and nearly ran me over—I chose to chalk up to experience. I walked away from it (literally and figuratively). I enjoyed learning how to drive one, and I like knowing I can do it if required. But I always had a sense of dread on a motorcycle. Portending perhaps, and a good reminder to trust your gut. If something consistently feels wrong, avoid it.

One of my favorite days ever was a Wednesday in December 2015 when I went skiing by myself. I was on a business trip in Banff, Alberta. I had decided to stay one more day and ski Banff Sunshine. I had been back living in Ontario for many years, and I always took advantage of time out west to enjoy the outdoors.

It was a very snowy December that year and the ski conditions were uncharacteristically good for so early in the season. I got up early, packed up the rental car, and drove out of Banff. It is one of my favorite areas in the world, but I was a little scared. The road was empty; I was by myself. It was snowing heavily. I was in a sedan not properly equipped for snowy mountain roads. I finally got to the parking lot to find it spattered with a few cars and people. I bought my day pass, got in a gondola by myself, and rode up the mountain through the clouds of snow to a clear blue sky and the ski area. Got on a chairlift by myself,

*At one point, I realized that if I wiped out and hurt myself, I could be waiting a very long time for help. It reminded me to take it easy, be present, and invest attention in my well-being.*

went up to the top, and proceeded to ski by myself for the whole day. I saw other people skiing, riding the lifts, having lunch. But I never waited in line, never sat with anyone on the lift. Again, exhilarating and scary. At one point, I realized that if I wiped out and hurt myself, I could be waiting a very long time for help. It reminded me to take it easy, be present, and invest attention in my well-being. I had to notice when my legs were tired, when I was out of breath. Take a break. There wasn't anyone else there to take care of me but me. Those are important life moments.

When I was going out with my aforementioned boyfriend, I had many of these adventures. He was an elite hang-glider pilot, fantastic skier, all-round high-level extreme sport kind of guy. I remember us going to a hang-gliding weekend festival and tournament in Golden, BC, with a bunch of like-minded folks. I met people from all over the world who came to BC to hang-glide with the best. We would travel to the top of a mountain and find a grassy outcropping covered in hang-gliders and tents and 4x4s and people. A lineup would be created for launching order. Once Ross launched, it was my job to drive the 4x4 and stay connected on the walkie-talkie to see where he might land, maybe an hour or more later. So much fun! I was driving through incredible terrain by myself. Scary and exhilarating. I once turned a corner and saw a pack of wild horses in a meadow. Just being horses in the Rockies. Wow.

Back in Toronto, I learned to hang-glide at Centennial Park in Etobicoke, from a cool older guy who just lived life full on. There were about ten of us in the class. He taught us about meteorology and aerodynamics and how to manage your mind to stay calm when things got stressful. As graduates of the program, we spent a weekend in upstate New York to experience flying bigger mountains. Certainly, not the Rockies, but it felt like it to me!

I also learned how to sail. We raced Cal-20s in English Bay, usually in the rain. We rented forty-two-foot sailboats to go on trips throughout Georgia Strait and the Gulf Islands, and once, a week-long trip up the coast to Desolation Sound. Its name is apt. There were times when the depth-reader went blank, that's how deep the waters were. Large creatures lived down there. And we managed through crazy storms and had to batten the hatches. I now know what that means! And we sailed alongside dolphins and orcas and other sea creatures; we caught fresh crab and moored in silent coves.

All of these experiences gave my life such flavor and color and texture and perspective. I am grateful for every single one.

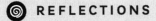

## ◎ REFLECTIONS

When in your life have you taken advantage of learning something new, having a new experience?

What have you learned and discarded? Why?

How do you determine your comfort levels with risk and reward?

Where does your reckless meter kick in?

What would you like to reconnect to or reintroduce in your life?

What else do you want to try?

What do you need to do in order to begin?

What's holding you back?

# The
# Corporate
# Gigs

*"And the day came when the risk to remain tight in a bud was more painful than the risk it took to blossom."*

ANAÏS NIN

**A**FTER A COUPLE of years working the series of random jobs I described earlier, I longed for the financial and intellectual rewards of working in the pharma industry, so I went back, with a role in specialty sales in the areas of neurology, rheumatology, and sports medicine. My territory was the Lower Mainland (Vancouver) up north to Whistler (and Whitehorse) and a bit of the interior (Kamloops, Okanagan Valley). I liked my job. I *loved* my territory. I loved having the financial freedom to do what I wanted when I wanted.

I continued to have a very active outdoor life, continued my artistic passion, and reconnected with my music life. I had dabbled in songwriting, playing guitar, and performing a few years earlier (home in Toronto) but I had since let it slide. I was curious to see how I might approach it differently now that I had traveled the world, relocated to a different environment, and generally had a somewhat different outlook on life (more on music later). This move back into corporate life also proved necessary to meet my future husband and father of my super awesome kid. (That story is queued up next.)

I was able to develop much deeper consultative selling skills in this role—dealing with physicians, nurses, pharmacists, and hospital bureaucracy—and was enjoying the connection of ideas, debate, service (helping patients), and blending the art and science of medicine and business. I had been in regular discussions about moving to the corporate head office back in Toronto, to take a promotion and advance my career, but I felt strongly about maintaining the fantastic life I had created in Vancouver.

A year later, a family tragedy changed all that and, thankfully, when I needed to move back home to the Toronto area, I was transferred immediately and promoted into my first head office role.

I spent eight years in the office, moving up and across various commercial roles, enjoying the variety, and especially the learning from the different people and perspectives I had access to. (Seeing the wizard behind the curtain is always fascinating to me.) What I didn't like was the political environment and the rigid belief that things had to move the way they always had—i.e., you do this job and then that job, and then this will happen and then that will happen. Also, there often seemed to be misalignment between the stated corporate values and leaders' actions.

I also experienced the very common reality of gender inequality and sexism during those years. In one clear-cut case, I applied for and was given a promotion.

The job was exactly the same as it had been for my predecessor, but I was given a lesser title along with a much lesser salary. There were also many instances where I was excluded from the important relationship-building aspect of career advancement. At the end of a day of meetings, the "boys" would all go play hockey together, go to strip clubs together, play and bond together. The junior sales guys and the executive leaders. There were ranking games to rate the attractiveness of the female leaders at the company, i.e., "Who is most fuckable?" Quite simply, this blatant sexism contributes to gender inequality and toxic work environments. Those involved may have had no idea they were contributing to deep discomfort on the part of many female colleagues—subordinates, peers, and superiors.

(It may be interesting for you to notice how you feel when you read this. What's going on in your self-talk bubble? Depending on your perspective, you may have very different reactions to this story. It is an important reflection in its own right.) Unfortunately, in spite of "respect in the workplace" policies and mandated online workshops, many of these practices continue.

The older I get, the less tolerant I am of bullshit—from individuals, institutions, systems, but also myself.

During the course of planning and implementing business strategies, I would, of course, ask why. "What about doing it differently?" "How could we be better?" "How could we be both values-driven *and* profitable?" I was

*The older I get, the less tolerant I am of bullshit— from individuals, institutions, systems, but also myself.*

curious to understand what the pros and cons were of running in a tightly regulated rigid straight line versus allowing room for freedom and curiosity and exploration. Surely there were pros and cons to both!

Again, due to personal circumstances (more on this in a minute) and a growing dissatisfaction with senior leaders' practice of values (i.e., lack thereof), I decided to move to the next stage: a new company, a sales management role, and a tidy little geography in which to work. Much-reduced travel. Home based and more available for the tot. My specific focus was leading an ever-changing sales team by attracting, developing, retaining, and promoting our key talent and ensuring our business goals were met at the same time.

I spent ten years in management—leading, coaching, driving business, managing performance, developing greater political astuteness, and deepening my understanding of the corporate ecosystem. I feel privileged to have worked for and with many incredible people for a company I respected and that afforded me even more professional opportunity and development—courses at business schools, certification programs, and private tailored development workshops. I will always be grateful for that. They provided me with the bedrock abilities to do the next thing.

## ◎ REFLECTIONS

Take ten minutes to graph your work journey. Include major milestones only.

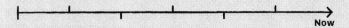

Mark the spots where curiosity led to learning and new experience. Mark the spots where you *wish* you had been more curious.

What might you have added to your knowledge, expertise, experience?

What can you still do now?

What do you still want to explore?

# Parenting as
# School of Life

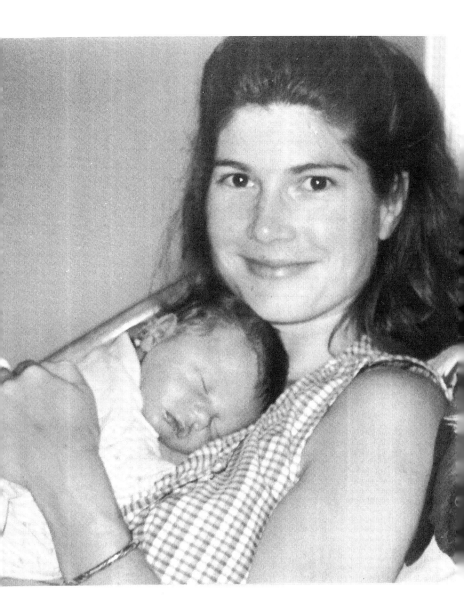

ONE OF THE most curious and uncertain things you can do is become a parent.

I was never the girl who dreamed of getting married and having a family. In fact, I cannot recall a single time when I could describe my best future life and who would be in it. I also cannot answer the common question "When you were little, what did you want to be when you grew up?" I seemed to relate most to an independent, uncertain, free, meandering existence.

However, as life rolled on, I got married, the biological clock struck twelve, and boom, I suddenly thought, "Yeah, let's do this."

Being present for the birth of my niece was likely another impetus. I was in love with her, and relating to this little creature came naturally to me. I wanted to give it a go. Ultimately it was curiosity that made me do it. I wanted to have the experience that billions of people have had and will have—now, before, and in the future.

_I find it curious when parents-to-be or parents-in-existence try to control everything—the gender, the timing of the birth, the timelines and game plans for the kid's life, the mud, the friends, the likes/dislikes. Let 'em be kiddies! Let go and stay curious._

(Side note: I believe it is of critical importance that we continue to fight for women's right to choose motherhood and not have it thrust upon us. This has vast social and economic ramifications.)

My curiosity about parenthood, and specifically giving birth and being a mother, led to the role I now most identify with. Being my son's mom is the most important role I have ever had and the one I feel most connected to. Without embracing uncertainty and curiosity, I would not have taken that fork in the road.

As my son grew, we experienced the different stages of the parent/child relationship—dependence, control, discipline, independence, interdependence, autonomy. I acknowledged that I didn't always have the answers. Using the perspective of curiosity has served me well. I asked better questions. I researched more broadly. I tested and validated approaches and assumptions. I failed and was curious about the failure. I admit my failures and regrets to him and ask for forgiveness.

We had a lot of fun together and a lot of adventures! We got a puppy when he was five, and that wonderful dog was with us for fifteen years. We traveled to family cottages and southern homes, along with my sister and her kids. We got involved with local hockey (him playing, me as team trainer, his dad as coach). He took piano for a couple years at my behest, and although he has a terrific ear and great voice, he never really got into music. He was a good trumpet player in middle school. I had to let it go—music was my jam (literally), not his. He is a thoughtful, sensitive, strong, and principled guy, fun and funny, loving and loyal to friends and family. Always was, still is.

Do I have any regrets? You bet. Some of my regrets were about decisions that were never in my control, but I wish I had been more evolved in terms of my reactions. I wish I had approached certain situations with more certitude, strength, and resilience. I wish I had had the wisdom I now have. Of course, there's the rub: you can't get it without going through it. That is also one of the toughest yet most critical factors of good parenting—you must let them fail, get hurt, and make mistakes in order for them to have the life experiences that, along with an open mind, enable wisdom. Same goes for the parent.

I feel truly blessed to have always had a great relationship with him, as a child and now as he enters adulthood. I like him as a person. I like hanging out with him. I'm still ferociously protective and am learning how to let go of one way of mothering him and shift into a different way—hopefully as a trusted advisor, sacred touchstone, a welcoming home of unwavering and unconditional love.

Curiosity is one of the main things I try to encourage my son to embrace. Keep learning. Ask questions. Be vulnerable. Know that you don't know it all (thank goodness!) and that's okay. Live your values.

As he was growing up, I tried to balance strong discipline with lots of flex. At one point, he was going through tough stuff at school, upheaval with his dad's new family,

*A state of wonder is*
*a wonderful thing.*
*State of wonder = full of wonder*
*Full of wonder = wonderful*

we had moved to a new home, and that can be a lot for a kid. So, even though he had his own room, he slept on a mattress on my bedroom floor for a few years. His own space but close to me. Discipline and flex.

I have always kissed him goodnight. When he's home, I still do. In fact, the tables are often turned, and since I now go to bed earlier, he comes to kiss me goodnight.

I find it curious when parents-to-be or parents-in-existence try to control everything—the gender, the timing of the birth, the timelines and game plans for the kid's life, the mud, the friends, the likes/dislikes. Let 'em be kiddies!

Let go and stay curious.

Let uncertainty teach you about your child and yourself.

## Rituals and Routines

Sometimes navigating change and life's challenges is just too much all at once. Rituals, routines, and practicing traditions help us manage the discomfort of too much.

Traditions don't have to be "big." Traditions are simply things that we do repeatedly with others that make us feel connection, comfort, and love.

Since my son was about ten years old, we have had a tradition of watching *Survivor* and eating homemade pizza together. Even though he is often away at university now, we still save the episodes and watch together when he is home. Along with homemade pizza. The recipe is quick and easy. Here it is.

## Homemade Pizza

1½ cups unbleached flour
1 teaspoon quick rise yeast
½ teaspoon salt
½ teaspoon sugar
½ cup warm water
2 tablespoons olive oil
toppings of your choice (tomato sauce, cheese, etc.)

Mix all dry ingredients in a large bowl. Mix about ½ cup warm water and about 2 tbsp olive oil in a cup. Add to the dry bowl and mix with your hands. Add more flour as required to make a soft dough.

Cover and let sit for about 20-30 minutes.

Preheat oven to about 485°F.

Take dough out of bowl and roll out on floured board. Roll until you like it. We make thin crust.

Sprinkle cornmeal on cookie sheet. Put your crust on the sheet and add your toppings. We usually keep it simple: tomato sauce, cheese, whatever additional toppings you like.

Bake for 10-12 minutes. Let sit for a few minutes before cutting.

Boom. Homemade pizza. These weekly (and now sometimes monthly) dates make me very happy.

During times of upheaval, find small ways to create ritual, routine, and tradition. It can bring meaningful balance to all that curiosity-induced action!

 **REFLECTIONS**

What traditions do you have?

What do you love about them?

What other traditions would you like to have?

How can you begin?

What value would it bring to your life? To your loved ones' lives?

What's stopping you?

# Privilege and Prejudice

*"Be kind. Everyone you meet is carrying a heavy burden."*

IAN MACLAREN

T HESE TWIN words—privilege and prejudice—are pretty loaded these days. They've always been around, loitering in the fray. It was a tidy background noise that some of us could tune out when it was inconvenient for us to think about it. And now they are front and center. The only invitation here is to take a breath and get curious about your place on the privilege continuum and how it might inform your implicit (unconscious) or explicit (conscious) biases.

Like a card hand, whaddya got?

- White

- Male

- Financially independent, or able to be

- Access to good health care

- Rights to your own body

- Educated

- Stable family unit

- Safe home

- Safe neighborhood

- A community that acknowledges your partner

- Voting rights

- Traditionally attractive

- Able-bodied

- You are represented in film, television, and print media

- You have the means to participate in activities like athletics, music, arts, or travel

- You have a "seat at the table"

Even the way this list is articulated likely comforts some and enrages others.

When I was asked to do some diversity and inclusion work recently, I had to do some inner work first and fully recognize the implicit biases I held and the privilege and prejudice I owned, regardless of my purported "woke" status. This is an important and large mess of yarn to unravel. Open-mindedness, curiosity, and non-binary thinking will be critical as we proceed to learn together and from each other.

I wrote this song years ago, but it seems even more apt now.

## "Smile and Wave"

A storm cloud's rolling in, you can feel it in the air,
inky blue on the horizon
Run for cover in the night, it never feels quite right
when your shelter's on a landmine
A hard rain's gonna fall, as Dylan said,
We can't save them all, we might as well be dead
The king and all his men just smile and wave
A message in a bottle, floating near the shore,
just out of reach and never opened
In a language we all speak, but we're running with
the weak, and a martyr seals his freedom
I just had a dream, Martin Luther said,
You could hear the people scream, they might as
well be dead
The king and all his men just smile and wave
Everything is clearer when it's far behind,
20/20 in the mirror
Trust your intuition, believe in the belief, that
consciousness is higher
Go give peace a chance, as Lennon said,
We used to sing and dance, now we might as well be dead
The king and all his men just smile and wave

 catherineharrison.com

## ◉ REFLECTIONS

Where does power reside in your family, neighborhood, workplace, city, country?

What power imbalances do you notice?

Where is your discomfort in this reflection? Any defensiveness? Any other feelings?

What will you do next to expand your knowledge about the struggles of others?

# The Piano

WHEN I WAS around five years old, I started piano lessons at a neighbor's house. I recall that I didn't particularly like it. The house smelled funny and they had a scary Doberman. That lasted a few months. A few years later, I continued my lessons with another piano teacher, Mr. Warner, who lived a few blocks away. I liked it better, I progressed further and even did the requisite piano recitals, but it wasn't something I yearned to continue. I don't remember this explicitly, but somehow even then I wanted to focus more on developing self-expression than rote technical performance.

I did, however, always gravitate to a piano if one should appear—hotel lobbies, homes, school and church auditoria. I would plunk away at simple melodies. There is something magical about a piano. Anyone can sit and begin striking notes and all of a sudden you are making music!

(A quick tangent: I believe music and art must be taught in all schools—public, private, whatever. There's a story about Winston Churchill during World War II. When he was asked to cut funding to the arts in order to support the war effort, he responded, "Then what would we be fighting for?" Whether this is appropriately ascribed or not, he was famously protective of the arts.)

In my first apartment in Toronto after university, I bought a digital piano so I could play with my headphones on and be respectful of the neighbors. I played like a guitar player—chords, percussively. I added a few Neil Young and Carole King piano tunes to my repertoire. When I say *added*, I mean I played them in my own rudimentary way, learning the instrument as I learned the songs.

When I eventually owned a home, I wanted a real piano. I wanted an upright piano for the living room. My budget was $2,000. I scoured the buy and sell ads, wandered through instrument consignment shops, and generally asked around. No luck.

One Sunday morning, I noticed a sale advertisement for a local piano dealership. They sold new and used pianos. I figured I would check it out, to learn more about what I was looking for and where I might find it if nothing else.

I walked in. A warehouse full of pianos. New, fancy, old, grand, uprights, parlor, digital. Overwhelming.

I asked a young salesman to help me. I described what I was looking for. We looked at a few pianos in proximity to where we were standing, near the back of the warehouse. I had a Goldilocks moment—each piano we tried didn't quite feel right, or sound right, or fit into the right price range.

*I had a Goldilocks moment—each piano we tried didn't quite feel right, or sound right, or fit into the right price range. Then he said, "Did you already look at the one near the front door?" I had not.*

Then he said, "Did you already look at the one near the front door?" I had not.

At the front door, a gorgeous, dark wood, upright grand piano. $1,999. It was a Bell piano built in Guelph, Ontario, in 1908. It was beautifully worn in all the right places. It was in terrific condition. The tone was fantastic. Sold.

I have had that piano since 2003. And the person who taught me the most about playing that piano was my friend, Mary, after breakfast one morning in 2004. And yes, Mary is Jeff Buckley's mom, whom I mentioned earlier. The circles continue.

---

◎ **REFLECTIONS**

How do you make room in your life for activities that are just for you?

How might you investigate adding more? What would need to shift?

What did you dislike as a child that you might want to retry?

# Genuine
# Curiosity and
# Asking Good
# Questions

*"Alice asked the Cheshire Cat, who was sitting in a tree, 'What road do I take?'*

*The cat asked, 'Where do you want to go?'*

*'I don't know,' Alice answered.*

*'Then,' said the cat, 'it really doesn't matter, does it?'"*

LEWIS CARROLL,
*ALICE'S ADVENTURES
IN WONDERLAND*

**W**HY DO WE put so much value on statements instead of questions? Culturally, we raise people to "know stuff." And then you have to repeatedly prove you "know stuff."

Flip it on its head. If you really want to lead, innovate, be more strategic and progressive, loosen your attachment to absolute knowledge and ask genuine, open-ended questions.

It's curious to me when I coach leaders that some will say, "Oh, you coaches just ask questions and never give the answers!" As if that's a bad thing. Some never get the value of tapping into their own innate creativity and self-sufficiency. Others get hooked on the thought partnership and really adapt, grow, expand, and move forward—individually and organizationally.

A great example of why we should keep asking questions ran in an article by Warren Berger ("The Power of Why and What If," July 2, 2016) in the *New York Times*: "The Polaroid story is my favorite: the inspiration for the instant camera sprang from a question asked in the mid-1940s by the three-year-old daughter of its inventor, Edwin H. Land. She was impatient to see a photo her father had just snapped, and when he tried to explain that the film had to be processed first, she wondered aloud, 'Why do we have to wait for the picture?'

 **REFLECTIONS**

Where can you ask more questions in your life?

What would you like to know more about?

How can you practice asking more and telling less?

How can you practice managing the self-talk bubble while you listen to the answers?

**Well done!** You followed your curiosity to see what the heck was upside down!

Now that you're here: Identify three things you are curious about. What one small step can you take today to follow that curiosity?

**The Thing I'm Curious About**

1.
2.
3.

**The One Small Step I Will Take**

1.
2.
3.

# The Muse
# and Muse-ic

THE MUSE is curiosity manifest. You must be curious to answer the call. What will happen? What will I create? Where do I begin? How will I know when it's done? Will this be a product or a process?

Although I love creating with pretty much anything (paint, crayons, rocks, yarn, fabric, wood... ), creating music is my anchor.

My musical journey is always different. Sometimes I wake up with something that comes out full form, all done; I just need to get out of the way and get it down on paper and through the guitar or piano. Other times it is a restlessness to work, to wrestle with the process of creating. To take a chord, a progression, a lyric, and mold, remold, smash it, play with it, leave it, come back to it. Until it's finished. Or good enough. Sometimes the song isn't finished, but my process is. Sometimes that is all that is required. To spend time on the process. To be in the moment. To learn something new. To struggle. To release. To let go. Sometimes, often times, that work leads to other outcomes—whether an artistic one (a different song) or a personal one (a certain aha moment, an awakening, a reflection, an insight).

My curiosity has served me exceptionally well in this facet of my life. So many profound life experiences and personal relationships have come from pursuing curiosity— and giving fear the finger!

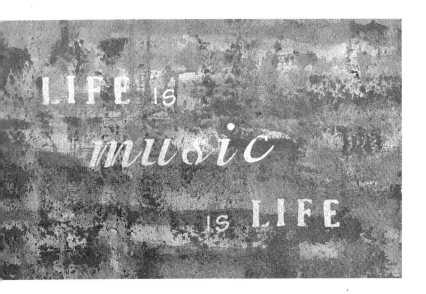

## Side Note

I wrote a song about this very thing—that is, following your curiosity and seeing what happens. Here are the lyrics:

## "Might Be Nothing"

It might be nothing, but it might be everything
It might be nothing, but it might be everything
Pick up a number, gonna call my baby
It might be nothing, but it makes me crazy
Little bit of loving gonna make it better
She can save you if you only let her
It might be nothing, but it might be everything
It might be nothing, but it might be everything
Hold onto something, gonna make my soul sing
Might be nothing, but it's pulling at the heart strings
Dance a little, love a little, revel in the sunshine
Might be nothing, but at least it's all mine
Don't go without kicking, make it through living and
you'll see
If they keep on winning, you're bruised in the beginning
But give it meaning and you'll see...

 catherineharrison.com

# The Story of
# My Guitars

*"My first love was the sound of guitar."*

BOZ SCAGGS

GREW UP AROUND guitars. My dad played guitar, and during family events at my grandma's house, he and his siblings would often pull out guitars and jam. I was marinated in it. As a young father in the late '60s, he was really into all the music that was available. We had records of Howlin' Wolf and CCR and Gordon Lightfoot and Bob Dylan and James Taylor and the Beatles and the Rolling Stones and the Carpenters and the Guess Who and Canned Heat and Tower of Power. He would play acoustic on his own and then jam with his friends, pulling out the Teles and the Strats.

I have always loved guitars. The look of them. The sound of them. The immediacy of them.

I first decided to play the guitar when I was thirteen. I used my dad's acoustic. I learned chords from a how to play guitar book, a slim beginner's guide. I didn't ask my dad for his advice or his help, nor did we jam together. The teen years are often the time when you begin to distance yourself from your parents to establish some individuality and independence, so I guess I was doing that. I learned a few Neil Young songs (requisite for a Canadian guitar learner) and "Greensleeves." Then I lost interest. I was very active in sports and school and socializing.

About ten years later, living in Toronto, I was dating a guy whose sister was a terrific singer-songwriter. She used to play for us. She was a great singer, and she played the acoustic in a way that really drew me in. Rhythmic, dynamic, simple yet powerful. I was intrigued to begin again. I borrowed her spare guitar for a while, then borrowed my dad's. I began writing my own songs. Writing lyrics came naturally to me as I had always been a writer: journals, poems, reflections, short essays. Also, writing my own songs ensured that I could play them—I chose the chords I knew (or made some up) and it was always in the right key.

On my twenty-second or twenty-third birthday, my dad gave me my first new guitar, a Samick six-string acoustic. This guitar was—and is—a great sounding guitar. With it in my life, I began to write more, play more, collaborate more. I began going to open mics at the Free Times Café on College Street and other local mainstays.

When I decided to take a stab at playing electric, I bought an imitation Sunburst Les Paul. Wow, it was different than playing an acoustic! I enjoyed the different sonic emotion it provided during the writing process. Playing electric, with reverb and distortion, I tended to write different, darker lyrics.

In 1992, while living in Vancouver, I bought a new Fender Telecaster (for those of you who care, it was Japanese Thinline) and a cheap Peavey amplifier (no hecklers, please). I eventually bought a Fender Hot Rod Deluxe tube amplifier (and a few more beautiful amplification machines—thanks CC!). I still have that Tele (and those amps) and I can't believe it is considered vintage itself!

As for the guitar I now play most often, it's my 1973 Giannini Craviola six-string acoustic. This guitar used to belong to my aunt's boyfriend (in 1973). I think his name was John. My dad bought it from him (later in the '70s). You can spot this guitar throughout our family photo albums. Although I loved my Samick, I had always loved my dad's Giannini, and over the years, I would pester him to lend it to me and he would. Eventually he just gave it to me outright, as he wasn't playing much anymore. This Brazilian guitar is known for its iconic shape and Brazilian rosewood fret board (guitar geeks unite!); it plays like a dream and sounds bigger than it looks.

I have bought and sold many guitars. I still have a Godin twelve-string semi-acoustic, a Gibson SG, and a Hawaiian-made ukulele. I gave the imitation Sunburst to a friend's kid and sold a rarely played, almost new Godin 5th Avenue Kingpin Archtop (it deserved to be played often and loved fully). The ones I will always keep, without question, are the Samick, the Giannini, the Tele, the Godin semi-acoustic, and the bass.

Ah, the bass.

We begin another series of random paths taken. Saying yes to collaborative creative projects, meeting friends of friends, and collecting conversations. In 2010 I met the author Richard Scarsbrook. We chatted about writing and music and other common interests. He was planning a launch party for his next book, *The Monkeyface Chronicles*. He wanted a musical evening: readings from the novel interspersed with carefully curated songs to bring the story to life. He was really taken by one of the tunes I had played at the most recent Buckley tribute, "Yard of Blonde Girls" (Clark/Kramer/Lorre). He asked if I'd be interested in playing it as part of his upcoming book launch party, also at the Rivoli where we'd had many of the Buckley shows. This much-loved Toronto venue was frequented by local and international musicians, as well as iconic events like when the Kids in the Hall first performed. I said, "Sure," and the gig went on as planned. Great group of people, fun band, great night!

Subsequent to that show, the folks in the band decided we would continue playing together, collecting a cover or two from each musician. Then our bass player needed to quit the band (as I recall she was having a baby). Someone said, "Why don't you move to the bass chair, Catherine?" I didn't play the bass. After much debate, it was deemed prudent for me to learn. And I thought, "Well, hey, why not? I love the bass too! That would be fun." Not like it was a (famed Toronto venue) Massey Hall gig. We were rehearsing and jamming and having fun.

*I have always loved
guitars. The look of them.
The sound of them.
The immediacy of them.*

Many folks think of bass as being simple to play. Only four strings! And bass players certainly don't seem as busy as those lead guitar players! Often it's not even thought of at all; it's just part of the background. Well, I'm here to confirm that it's tougher than it looks. If the bass is off, the whole band is off. I had to get good at making solid time and simple, grounding notes that served the song. I borrowed a friend's bright blue P bass (thanks TL!) and learned the songs for that gig. I think we only did one show as a band but had a lot of really fun rehearsals. I played enough to want to play more. I wanted my own bass.

Professional bass-playing friend in tow, I ventured to Capsule Music on Queen Street West. I wanted a good-sounding, reasonably priced, used bass. We were focusing on feel and tone. We spent more than an hour trying out different basses, humming and hawing. Then he saw it. Hanging above my head was a red, short-scale bass with a white pick guard. It was perfect. A 1975 Fender Musicmaster, the younger sister of the Mustang. And I bought it and I loved it and I love it to this day.

It always reminds me of that movie *The Red Violin*, about a beautiful antique violin and its journey from Italy to Montreal over four centuries and through all its owners. I really wish my bass could talk and tell me about its journey through different owners, and gigs and living rooms and used guitar shops and back seats and dusty closets and basements. Who knows what tales it could tell?

## Side Note

I tend to buy things when I'm going through a relationship breakup. And not frivolous things like clothing, shoes, or knickknacks. Substantial things like guitars, pianos, cars, cottages. It's like I'm finally giving into something I'd wanted but didn't allow myself. Through the emotional turmoil of a breakup, it's as though I desperately want to reconnect with myself, the self that somehow went wayward during the relationship.

 **REFLECTIONS**

What are the stories of your favorite things?

What memories might they hold?

What are your hopes for them "after you"?

# Getting Stuff Done

*"Life isn't about finding yourself.*
*Life is about creating yourself."*

ATTRIBUTED TO

GEORGE BERNARD SHAW

**H**OW CAN we leverage curiosity to get what we want? Let's say you begin with a clear vision of some thing you want. It's time to put a plan in place, using the old SMART goal model: specific, measurable, attainable, realistic, and time-based. By adding details to your plan, you up the odds of it actually coming to fruition. You can't just sit on the couch reflecting on your vision, waiting for it to happen. You need to take action.

When creating your plan, start by taking inventory of the resources available to you. Get really curious about your answers. Take your time. Ask yourself the following questions:

- What do I need to achieve my goal? What do I currently have that can help me?

- What skills/resources will I need? How can I secure them?

- Who do I know? Who do I need to meet? Who can I ask for help?

- What changes do I need to make to my schedule to achieve my vision of success?

Your resource inventory will help you map out a plan to reach your goals. The next step is to execute your plan. Even if things don't go exactly as you imagined, you will likely find that the universe conspires to help you achieve your vision. Especially if you remain open and curious along the way.

You must learn to say yes to opportunities as they present themselves (like my Rivoli experience I shared earlier).

The term *synchronicity* was coined by Swiss psychiatrist Carl Jung and refers to "meaningful coincidences." The appearance of synchronicity is the result of the well-known psychological phenomenon of confirmation bias (there it is again!): we more easily notice and remember things that confirm our beliefs than those that do not. Our brains are very good at making connections and noticing important data in seemingly random patterns. Positive = more positive, negative = more negative. It is the context of the glass half full/half empty cliché. What you see is your reality, and your reality then follows suit.

Some of the most life-changing and direction-changing events have happened in my life simply by saying yes to an opportunity, and that triggered a cascade of experiences that helped shape my life, ultimately bringing to me what I wanted all along, or something better, or different. Some things I couldn't have even known about before

———————

*When opportunity knocks,
get curious. Explore
possibilities. Explore where
uncertainty may take you.*

———————

they showed up. Some would say that's luck. I know better. When opportunity knocks, get curious. Explore possibilities. Explore where uncertainty may take you.

I have a fridge magnet that says, "Stress is when your heart says no and your mouth says, 'Sure, I'd be glad to!'" You must consciously identify what you say yes to that hinders your ability to realize your vision. For example, say *no* to doing the bake sale (unless you *love* doing the bake sale). Say *no* to any toxic people in your life, the naysayers who like to sabotage your efforts. They are exhausting. Say *no* to social events and online activities that take you away from your vision path. Say *no* to doing everything for everyone else (parents, children, spouses, friends, coworkers, etc.) at the expense of your vision. You will all be better off for it.

You may even find it useful to get curious about why you feel such stress if/when you consider saying no to people. Why?

Conversely, I have noticed that I say no a lot to people who offer to help me. What's up with that? So, I am learning to catch myself in the act, and then say, "Yes, thanks." When I choose to accept offered help, I am allowing myself to accept that I don't need to be responsible for everything, all the time.

What do you want and why do you want it? Make sure you want it for the right reasons. Sometimes what we want is not what *we* want, but what *others* want us to want (or worse, what *we think* other people want us to want).

When you align what you want with the limitless resources available to you, and stay curious about how it might play out, *imagine what might happen.*

 **REFLECTIONS**

What are you passionate about?

What are you merely interested in?

What do you really dislike doing but still do?

What are you good at?

What would you like to be better at?

What is the next step?

# The Next Thing

*"The secret of life, though, is to fall seven times and to get up eight times."*

PAULO COELHO, *THE ALCHEMIST*

ISILLUSIONED WITH THE corporate world, and specifically my immediate superiors' choices, actions, and behaviors, I decided to call it a day and leave the industry. There's a whole other backstory here, but quite frankly I don't want to relive it, and there are still individuals gainfully employed that I choose not to call out here. Bottom line—my belief system was rocked, and I couldn't work for a company where hypocrisy reigned supreme.

Okay. So, all of a sudden, for the first time in almost twenty years, I was unemployed.

I had put myself in the fortunate financial position of being able to take time off and figure out what to do next. I needed time to heal, to reflect, to investigate possibilities. I did just that for six months.

I journaled, I talked with people. I put myself through a rigorous, self-constructed curriculum of reading—leadership, industrial psychology, behavioral economics, neuroscience, autobiographies, conscious capitalism—and talked with anyone anywhere about what they did for a living and why.

I decided that I loved business and, specifically, the humans in business. I had reached some pretty clear conclusions: people drive everything! The innovation, the creativity. Humans make the thing, sell the thing, buy the thing. They lead other humans to do their best work (or not). They can change the world (for better or worse). That good business is fundamentally all about connection, creativity, and communication.

I decided that I would hang out a shingle and see if anyone would hire me, as a consultant, to help facilitate the implementation of that philosophy, to support the development of individuals' abilities to connect, create, and communicate more effectively. I believed it would lead to healthier organizations with better talent strategy and more engagement that attract and support the right customers to grow the business in an ethical, thoughtful, holistic, and sustainable way.

I had to name my company. My sister said, "How about Purple Voodoo?" It had been the name of the production company I created during the Buckley show years to manage the income from the shows and cut checks to the charities. It was a silly little name, made up with a friend while skiing. I said, "Ridiculous... That doesn't sound like a serious business consulting company!" And then after months of trying to articulate what the company would stand for, and trying on many different names, from boring to clever, Purple Voodoo emerged as the perfect name.

*I decided that I loved business and, specifically, the humans in business. I had reached some pretty clear conclusions: people drive everything! The innovation, the creativity. Humans make the thing, sell the thing, buy the thing.*

Purple is the color of enlightenment, the crown chakra. It is the combination of two primary colors, red and blue, which are often seen as the yin/yang in describing dichotomies. Red is warmth, emotion, blood, and fire. Blue is cool, calm, rational, and logical. The idea that we all have both aspects and use them in various ways, to various degrees, was a core philosophy. How do we learn to leverage both sides of ourselves? Of each other? Voodoo (meaning *spirit*), I discovered, is an ancient spiritual practice that holds the individual accountable for their actions, while also keeping the community in mind. A perfect representation of my business consultancy!

Also, the tag line "connect, create, communicate" came from a split-second answer to a question about how to live your best life. I was listening to a podcast while exercising one day. The speaker was talking about how you could answer the standard meet-and-greet question "What do you do?" Instead of sharing about your paid job, you could reply with a deeper, more reflective "Who are you?" perspective. The speaker invited the audience to say the first word that came to mind. For me, it was immediate—those three words tumbled out of me, out loud. They not only inform the basis of what we do as a company, but who I am, what I do, and how I roll—in life, art, music, business.

So, I went for it. I tried and failed, tried and succeeded, learned where I should work and where I shouldn't. I honed my knowledge, skills, and focus. I invested in relationships that made me better through synergy, open-mindedness, collaboration. I continued to read, took courses, got certifications. I asked a lot of questions. I tried a lot of approaches. I failed a lot. I reflected a lot. I said yes a lot. I am learning to say no more to work or people that don't align with Purple Voodoo philosophy and methodology; it quickly becomes a Sisyphean effort to manifest any meaningful outcomes. What I love most about my current vocation is that I can constantly adapt, evolve, grow, and pivot to the external environment and support others in doing the same. Now and for the foreseeable future, learning to adapt will be learning to exist.

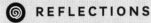

## ◉ REFLECTIONS

Identify a "big event" in your work life that forced you to make a radical change. Describe it in as much detail as possible.

What did you learn about yourself?

What did you learn about others? Who specifically?

What did the "big event" lead to?

How have you benefited from that catalyst even if it seemed negative at the time?

# Love

OW DOES CURIOSITY figure into this equation? It's simple: love drives curiosity, fear drives stagnation. Throughout my life, whenever I have managed to overcome fear, emotional pain, and patterned triggers to switch my perspective to be open and curious, I reconnect to love. And in reconnecting to love, to my true self, to my soul, I am able to explore and to grow and to expand. I am able to give generously of my time and energy, to myself and to others.

When I have allowed fear to dominate my thoughts and actions, it has prevented me from enabling my naturally curious state. It has prevented me from explorations of new experiences and new people and new awareness and insight. It gets me stuck in unhealthy places, relationships, jobs. Love actually enables me to let go, move forward, stay curious about unknown possibility.

Fear prevents. Love enables. As Kenny Werner said, "In fear, we expect. In love, we accept."

The pairing of love and curiosity has driven all my new relationships and has been a source of energy and sustenance for any relationships that have sustained over time. Any negativity that emerged in interactions within or even destruction of a relationship always came from fear. Sometimes it came from forgoing my naturally curious state and losing my authentic power. Sometimes it came from my selfishness and righteousness about independence and freedom. Sometimes it came from misalignment with my partner—one person rigid and restricting, the other open and expanding. Ultimately these relationships were unhealthy, toxic places that disabled my sense of self and resulted in deep emotional and spiritual trauma.

We all have core human needs: the need to be seen for who we are; the need to know we matter; the need to know we are loved.

Reflecting on those tough experiences, I've learned that I stopped being curious about what I needed to be whole and healthy, that I refused to look at what I was sacrificing to stay in the relationship. That is, what was I avoiding or ignoring based on fear of loss? Sometimes my fear of uncertainty kept me trapped in an unhealthy space where I became smaller and smaller. Love that only flows one way is not rooted in truth nor will it sustain well-being.

All of my business ventures, my artistic pursuits, my travels, and certainly my experiences as a mother can connect directly to curiosity and true love. Enabling curiosity allows us to ask empathic questions: How is the other truly feeling right now? Where might their behavior stem from? What pain might they be feeling right now? Is it possible to

*We all have core human needs: the need to be seen for who we are; the need to know we matter; the need to know we are loved.*

see myself in them and their behavior right now? How can I empathize with their perspective? What do I notice about myself and my habits and thinking patterns that may be contributing to this conflict or stagnation? What solution might there be that I am unwilling to notice?

When I am able to stay curious about myself and my condition and about the other person and their condition, I am able to stay connected to love. When I disconnect from curiosity, it is easy to connect to judgment, intolerance, impatience, and righteousness. And all of these perspectives stem from fear.

## ⊚ REFLECTIONS

Write down three things that might prevent you from being curious in love.

1. _____

2. _____

3. _____

Write down three things that keep you connected to fear and disable your innate curiosity.

1. _____

2. _____

3. _____

Think of a time when you allowed yourself the freedom, with childlike wonder, to embrace curiosity to connect to love and to overcome an interpersonal challenge. What specifically did you do, or not do, that helped support that curiosity?

How might this apply to the workplace?

# Love at
# First Sight

*"We do not create our destiny;
we participate in its unfolding."*

DAVID RICHO

**Y**UP, HAD IT, married it. The relationship didn't last more than a few years, but the partnership did—we had a wonderful child and raised him, for the most part, together while apart.

The L.A.F.S. was necessary in order for us to have *that specific* child. When I saw him across the room at a business meeting and thought, "I want to marry that guy," it was purely universal guidance. It sure didn't make any sense and yet, in hindsight, it did.

Cool, eh?

We are still great friends, respect and care for each other, and enjoy watching *that specific* child become a super awesome adult. Thank you, SL.

## ◉ REFLECTIONS

When have you allowed yourself to make split-second decisions that didn't make sense and yet produced positive life-changing outcomes?

# Patterns

*"No society can understand itself without looking at its shadow side."*

GABOR MATÉ

WAS BORN INTO a tumultuous time that would symbolize the rest of my childhood and inform, filter, and color my adult experiences. Family secrets, lies, being told not to feel or see what I was feeling or seeing—because children were not supposed to see, feel, or question things that adults don't want to talk about, deal with, or reveal (due to their own fear and discomfort).

When you think about it, the majority of us humans were born during some sort of non-utopian situation, likely to parents who weren't completely evolved emotionally, psycho-socially, et cetera. And that can't help but influence our adult experiences. That's life. However, as adults, we can all choose to own it, learn about it, and use it as a starting point for reflection, growth, awareness, and accountability to move forward differently. (See the section on storytelling, page 197.)

Don't get me wrong. I had lots of happy times too. And I love my parents very much. As a knowledgeable adult, I can see that they were doing the best they could, as young parents with their own multigenerational stuff going on, and there just wasn't the kind of access to information about raising kids in an emotionally stable, psychologically safe environment as there is now. There were a lot of cultural normative myths in place. It doesn't discount, however, the impact that those experiences had on me as a young child, an older child, a teenager, and young adult.

Perhaps not surprisingly, later in life, I eventually found a man just like my dad, who I loved very deeply. In the good times, just like my dad, he was smart and charming and funny and incredibly talented, someone with whom I had a deep soul connection. However, just like my dad, alcohol was a central catalyst to his dark side. Just like my dad, he had a one-sided cruel approach to emotional discomfort and relationship conflict. Just like my young dad, he was enmeshed with his family of origin and wasn't prepared to see us as a new prioritized family unit. And just like my mom, I had to eventually leave the man whom I loved the most because it wasn't healthy for me to remain. It's so interesting to reflect on negative patterns that we find comforting. As difficult as it is to experience them, we seek them out and participate in them, until we learn our lessons and choose to move forward again, curious about what might lay ahead.

What is most curious about this situation is why I didn't listen to my gut when, even early on, mean-spirited comments and lack of empathy and kindness were major red flags. I mean, this wasn't my first rodeo. I had been

*Negative early experiences shape our psychological development and impact our belief system—about the world and ourselves.*

married already and I was in my forties. That's where I had to get curious about cultural expectations and norms (single woman bad!), multigenerational trauma and patterns (even bad patterns are familiar and comfortable), and a deep sense of low self-worth (that voice that tells you to just put up with it—try harder!). I felt stuck. I wasn't in a healthy relationship but I didn't want to lose "love." Of course, there are different kinds of love. Although I very much loved him, and he loved me in his own way, it wasn't ever going to be the kind of mutually respectful, supportive, and emotionally intimate partnership I was yearning for. I did deep work to shatter the illusion, see it for what it really was, and move forward in my life—cultural expectations and norms be damned. (More on this experience in "When It's Time to Go," page 185.)

Fortunately, my dad began learning to deal with his demons in midlife and softened; he was more and more able to notice and make better choices about his behavior, especially with us, the ones he loved most. I am forever grateful that we had a wonderful relationship (and he got to be part of my son's life) before he died. I wish we had had more time to continue that journey together.

As you look in the patterns in your own life and your own relationships, you may come to some startling discoveries. Give yourself permission to step into the discomfort, and be courageous enough and vulnerable enough with yourself to acknowledge what really happened. And that it's not your fault. Negative early experiences shape our psychological development and impact our belief system—about the world and ourselves. If, as children, we experienced any neglect, abuse, bullying, or regular punishment, we solidify the belief that we are "bad." If we fail to meet the expectations of our parents, our community, feel like the "odd one out," it triggers a constant feeling of disconnection. And if we don't receive love, affection, warmth, encouragement, and support, we can feel like we don't matter.

True, you may have played a role in keeping the pattern going. As you have grown up and moved through life, you may not have known how to step out of the well-worn track of your relational pathology. The first step is simply seeing it. When you name it, when you openly call it out, you take some of the energy away from the negative attachments and may then reinvest that energy in cultivating your own sense of self—self-love, self-advocacy, self-acceptance, self-fullness—and build up from there.

## ◉ REFLECTIONS

Where might you get curious about your human experience from age zero to *now*?

What do you notice in terms of filters and patterns?

What negative experiences or feelings might you be avoiding?

Where might you go next?

Where do curiosity, compassion, and accountability coexist?

# When It's Time to Go

*"Don't be afraid of losing people.*
*Be afraid of losing yourself*
*trying not lose someone."*

UNKNOWN

YOU GET OLDER, you think you know all the answers when it comes to relationships. Yet I learned some of my toughest lessons not so long ago.

I recently left a relationship to save my life. It sounds extreme, doesn't it? I wasn't being physically beaten nor did I fear for my life (although it began to feel that way). However, it was affecting my health. It was affecting my sense of self. And when one considers the whole human being—the emotional, physical, psychological—you cannot disconnect those things from each other. The individual and the environment are interconnected. The mind and the body are interconnected. If you do not express your truth, your authentic self, that misalignment and disconnectedness will go within and cause illness. To quote Dr. Gabor Maté from his book *When the Body Says No*, "automatic and compulsive concern for the needs of others while ignoring your own is a major risk factor for chronic illness." In that relationship, I was more concerned with supporting his emotional health than my own.

I had never been more in love and felt more myself with someone; at the same time, I had never been treated so poorly or felt so alone. Loneliness within a relationship is the toughest of all the lonelies. Of course, early on there were many signs that I chose to ignore. That is also the opposite of curiosity—denial.

This relationship afforded me a crystal-clear opportunity to witness firsthand multigenerational trauma, in another person and in myself. Many of us are impacted by multigenerational trauma and don't even know it. This is one of the most tragic and heartbreaking realities: hurt people hurt people. When secrets and feelings are kept hidden and self-worth is kept broken, true self-actualization is impossible. When emotional fluency is not taught, cultivated, and celebrated, intimacy is impossible.

It was also an opportunity to learn more about how misalignment in belief systems is a root cause of dysfunction, and ultimately results in untenable relationships. One belief system is that power is a win/lose endeavor. That is, if someone is winning, you are losing and vice versa; it's a zero-sum game. It necessitates control, dominance, and competition. It does not support a mutually loving, trusting, supportive partnership, romantic or otherwise. The other belief system is that power is about mutuality and cocreation. It is about growth and expansion and curiosity. It necessitates openness, vulnerability, and empathy. It's interesting to note that a relationship that has these two opposing belief systems in play results in frustration and

*If one cannot discuss issues directly with love, with transparency and vulnerability, it is not possible to cocreate love, trust, support, growth, consciousness. It's just two people together, not a collaborative unit.*

dis-ease for both parties—they are literally living in two separate realities. They see the world, including the relationship, through very different lenses.

And so, how do you resolve it? Well, if one person remains in the power-over belief system, there is no way to resolve it. Mutuality doesn't fit in that system. A decision must be made: to accept the illusion and a suboptimal life experience, or to move on, to move forward, with vulnerability, curiosity, and love.

What if you still love the person and can intellectually understand where they're coming from? What if you can even understand *why* they behave the way they do? Choosing to leave a relationship is like this: imagine trying to deal with a wounded animal (a lion, let's say). You may love the animal and understand why it is lashing out and being aggressive, but you still don't want to put yourself in harm's way by going into the cage. It's heartbreaking and difficult, but you make the decision to leave it alone for your own well-being.

If one cannot discuss issues directly with love, with transparency and vulnerability, it is not possible to cocreate love, trust, support, growth, consciousness. It's just two people together, not a collaborative unit.

When couples are struggling, they are often told to reach out for support. I connected with a couples' counsellor and got support in terms of what I needed to do, learn, try in order to grow. I was also advised to reach out to our community—that is, our friends and family. We had been together for many years and our families and social circles were integrated. So, I did. I shared what was happening and asked for support and help. Nobody wanted to "get involved." "You guys just have a communication issue." Unfortunately, this is often the "support" individuals get while dealing with verbal or emotional abuse: "Just learn to communicate better!"

Avoidance is how social systems perpetuate painful cycles. Keep the secrets secret. Pretend everything's okay. Don't ask anyone to do, think, or feel anything that's uncomfortable. Don't look under the rock and see the festering disease. Of course, those decisions lead to illness within the body or the system—family, company, community, nation—whether it be mental or physical.

Please note: experts confirm that verbal/emotional abuse doesn't always lead to physical abuse, but physical abuse is always preceded by verbal/emotional abuse. Get professional help as soon as you feel you need to.

For me, the most interesting aspect of my relationship was its duality. I was the most present, loving, selfless, and committed I have ever been. The connection was the deepest I have ever felt. And it was the most negative, toxic, and hurtful relationship experience I have endured.

It was like taking all of my love experiences, tumbling them together, and showing me, "Okay, you might be ready to do your best, after years of not doing your best, but we will give you someone who cannot or will not be able to meet you there." Wow. Mind blown. For all of the relationships

*"When someone shows you who they are, believe them."*

MAYA ANGELOU

where maybe I was unempathetic to the other person's perspective, K-A-R-M-A lassoed my heart and dragged it across the shattered glass. I had never left a relationship still in love, still deeply loving. This was a massive personal growth opportunity—to begin to self-advocate, set boundaries, to leave with empathy, to observe, to notice, to hold boundaries, to forgive and move forward.

Have you ever had to give up something you love? I mean really, truly, deeply love? And yet you know it's not good for you? One of my teachers used this analogy: you're looking for a car, you find the perfect car. It's the right color, the right model, the right year, the interior is in perfect shape, the sound system is amazing, it's got all the bells and whistles. You love it! You love the way it looks! You love the way it feels! You decide to buy it. And then the guy selling it says, "Oh, by the way, it doesn't come with any brakes."

You say "Wha?!" Yeah, the only problem is it doesn't come with any brakes. Here's the question: Do you still buy it? Most people would answer, "Of course not!"

I had chosen the superficial aspects of physical attraction, some common interests, and having fun over the deeper qualities of kindness, emotional intimacy, and a shared desire to grow in consciousness, individually and together.

Then I got curious—why *did* I put up with it? If I couldn't change him or his belief systems, why was I putting myself in harm's way, over and over? That curiosity finally led to the acceptance that nothing was going to change. I needed to be responsible for creating a healthy environment for me. As they say, you can't change the people around you, but you can change the people around you.

I will always regret staying as long as I did and marinating in such a negative atmosphere. I wasn't living my best life, nor being my best self: I wasn't being the best mother, daughter, friend, artist, entrepreneur that I could be. I had to be accountable and get curious about what to do next. What was possible? What were the options?

Sometimes that's what happens in life. You find people, places, or things that look good and feel good and you think, "This is it, this is awesome, I love this." And then you realize that a fundamental component is missing. Something that is necessary for your health and well-being. In those situations, one must learn to self-advocate and move away from that situation, however possible.

It was the duality of the relationship I am now so curious about. It gave me some of the things I wanted, but few of the things I needed. And, therefore, it invites me to reflect, consider, muse, unpack, explore all that I thought I knew about myself. Fascinating.

## ◎ REFLECTIONS

Where in your life did you ignore your own messages? Are you ignoring any now?

Where could curiosity and open-minded exploration have served you to make healthier choices?

Where have your patterns helped you? Hindered you? What do you notice now?

How have you participated in your relationships? What have you learned?

How have you contributed to your negative experiences? What might you do next time?

# Personal Power
# and Storytelling

*"We seldom realize, for example, that our most private thoughts and emotions are not actually our own. For we think in terms of languages and images which we did not invent, but which were given to us by our society."*

ALAN WATTS

"**W**HO AM I, really?"

It can be scary to ask this question. And it can be fascinating and important and life-affirming.

Sometimes we suffer from imposter syndrome—when we don't accept our strengths and accomplishments for what they are but rather downplay them due to a deep-seated belief that we aren't worthy. It is often accompanied with pervasive anxiety and stress about "being found out," or not ever being enough. How do we get curious, without judgment, about what's behind that?

There is always an opportunity to reconnect to who you really are, in all its messy and variable glory.

Struggle is the presence of something we don't want or the absence of something we do want.

Humans relate to stories. All world religions are based on stories, deemed sacred, mythological, or absurd. History is all based on stories—always someone's perspective of what happened (usually the victor's). The fact is we all use storytelling to explore the human condition and try to make sense of the world around us.

As soon as we're born, we start creating our story. At the beginning of our lives, we have no choice but to learn our story from our parents, our communities, our entertainment, our cultures. And we indoctrinate those stories into our identities and then live tethered to those same narratives, whether they serve us or not. Everyone, including ourselves, has a solid opinion about who we are, what we're good at, bad at, what we should or shouldn't do.

We all have triggers that lead to our own storytelling. Something happens, or someone does something, that triggers our survival mechanism. And we immediately craft a story that helps us cope and proceed. But how do these stories really help us? Oftentimes they hinder our ability to move forward with personal power and grace. We internalize and perpetuate our own limitations.

However, as we become adults, we have the choice to challenge those stories, to reframe and redesign them, to create new pathways of opportunity. To choose how we live, what we say, do, and feel. Everyone has a dark space somewhere in their lives. It can either define us forever or enable and empower us to grow, expand, and learn.

 **REFLECTIONS**

How might you get curious about yourself and accept, use, and leverage those insights? Ask yourself:

- Where am I my most authentic self?

- Is there more than one area?

- Who tells me what I can or cannot be?

- Am I an imposter? Who decides?

- Do I ever give my power away?

- Who decides my worth?

- Can I learn more about social constructs, human psychology, brain evolution and understand it, decode it, and use it to my advantage, instead of unconsciously adding to my suffering?

- What will be written about me in my obituary? What might be missing that I would want to include?

- Think of some stories about yourself and your life. I don't mean "remember that time when . . ." stories, but the stories about who you really are, deep down. Whose opinions do you still use as a filter through which you see yourself and your value? Whose voices do you hear? What are they saying?

You might say to yourself:

- Hmmm. Interesting!

- Where did that come from?

- How is it true?

- How might it not be true?

- How might it shift my perception of what is happening here?

- How is it connecting or disconnecting me from the other(s) in the situation?

These reflections can be heavy! As you consider your answers, if you are feeling any serious discomfort or anxiety or are reconnecting to trauma, reach out to a supportive professional.

# Leadership

*"I refuse to believe that you cannot be both compassionate and strong."*

JACINDA ARDERN

OFTEN GET HIRED to fix people. Fix them individually, fix their groups, fix their behavior, attitudes, and ultimately improve their output. I get hired by senior managers to fix the problems below them. Based on my experience as an employee in small, medium, and large organizations, and these days as an unbiased outsider, my conclusion is that it is often the leaders themselves who need the repair job and who could most benefit from self-reflection.

A critical success factor for leadership of any kind is the willingness and ability to engage in self-reflection, to honestly and courageously ask yourself, "How am I contributing to this situation?" Even with enlightened leaders, the questions often asked of me are "How can I support my people through *their* development, enlightenment, change?" or "What could I be doing differently to facilitate *their* progress and growth?"

The bottom line is that *you* are contributing, like it or not. No grey area here. The question is *how*. Ask yourself honestly, candidly, "How am *I* contributing to this situation?" Are you enabling your own beliefs, attitudes, assumptions, judgments, or success ideology to limit your understanding of those you lead? Have you ever said any of the following statements? "Well, when *I* was in that position..." "*This* is what motivates people... It motivated me!" "They're just whining!" "They don't understand the big picture!"

A growth-focused, open mindset paired with the courage and curiosity to look within and do the hard work of self-reflection are the ultimate qualities to being a great leader, whether it's in business, community, family, or personal relationships. Before you look outward, first look inward and ask yourself:

- Have I made it crystal clear what is expected of the individual/team?

- Have I shared my goals and challenges?

- Do I share the big picture?

- Have I ensured adequate resources are in place?

- Have I cultivated a learning environment where curiosity and sharing is encouraged?

- Have I provided timely and constructive feedback on a regular basis?

- Have I secured the most appropriate training and coaching for the required skills?

- Have I created a safe environment to fail, to learn, to grow?

- Have I checked in to see what motivates others?

- Have I sought regular feedback for myself and other senior leaders?

- Do my actions line up with my words? Am I walking the talk?

- Is my finger always pointed outward, or do I take responsibility for the situation?

- Do I make time for my people? Am I accessible and present when they need me?

- Do I facilitate development through meaningful dialogue, coaching, and support?

If you're going to spend time and money away from growing your business to focus on your team, you must also focus on self-reflection. You must have regular, meaningful conversations. You must engage and energize your people to collaborate and discuss new ways of approaching challenges and opportunities. You must ensure there is an always-present platform for sustainable connection and accountability, not just a few times a year.

In fact, it is critical that you take time away from tactical activities that drive your business and invest time, money, and energy in the real stuff—the foundational aspects upon which everything else is built. The data

*Prioritize supporting your employees and cultivating true connection, and do the self-reflection required to model this behavior with your team.*

continues to emerge showing the profound impact this deeper work can have on the bottom line. So, where one may have seen an either/or scenario, in fact, the two are directly and intricately connected. It has been proven that leaders who take the time to invest in their people get better results. Employee engagement impacts every other key performance indicator you care to measure. And that is good for business.

Research conducted by Gallup has proved that organizations with high levels of employee engagement report 22 percent higher productivity. In addition to this, strong employee engagement can provide a number of positive outcomes for the employees and customers. For example, organizations with high engagement have double the rate of success than those with low engagement. Engaged employees see the connection between day-to-day work and the larger mission of the organization. The employees are attentive and vigilant and there is lower absenteeism and turnover. The quality of work and employee health improves and there are fewer safety incidents.

When employees feel connected to organizations, we all know they are more involved and productive. However, engagement can be difficult to measure, as it often means different things to different people. The goal for leaders is to inspire their employees to do their best work. Leaders need to create a culture that inspires, empowers, and engages, thereby enabling the best work to emerge.

My favorite boss was my sales manager when I was a pharma rep in British Columbia. He was clear, honest, transparent, supportive, fun. He established all of this in our second interview together, when after an hour of discussing my candidacy (less than optimal for the position) and how I could contribute to the team's performance and leverage my previous experience and knowledge, he said, "Okay, you're hired. But if you have been shitting me, I'll be the first one in line to pull the chute." It may sound harsh, but I loved it! He was basically saying, "I trust that what you've been saying to me is true. I will give you a chance. I am going to bat for you. And I take honesty and hard work seriously. Don't betray this trust." And he remained a steadfast supporter of my career from that moment on. In fact, I used a similar line with my own hires once I became a leader. Being open, honest, real, authentically human and vulnerable, yet crystal clear about expectations, is paramount to my leadership style. That is why I left my corporate job: I was being asked to be nebulous and lie and play games with my people. Nope, not for me.

In a terrific article by Stacey Barr, "Can You Prove How Well Your Organization Is Performing?" she articulates the risk leaders take when they fear transparency and remain willfully ignorant of their contribution to the culture of the organization. The concept of gaming emerges as the way leaders leverage confirmation bias in a company, by finding what they want to find and seeing what they want to see. Ultimately nothing changes and performance continues to stagnate, or worse.

Be honest with yourself. Spend some time self-reflecting. Check in with your self-talk. Recognize the power of influence when you let go of the need to control. Attend training meetings with your people. Engage in follow-up discussions. Listen to what they tell you and collaborate to explore new solutions. Commit to the coaching sessions in your calendar (leaders are often the ones who cancel coaching regularly—"Just too busy!"). Make your leadership development a priority.

Prioritize supporting your employees and cultivating true connection, and do the self-reflection required to model this behavior with your team. Empower them to access and leverage the best in themselves and each other. Take it seriously. If you don't have time for it, you don't have time for maximizing results, productivity, efficiency, innovation, stability, and growth in your organization. My priority was always my people. I set firm boundaries for work/life balance but was always accessible to support, coach, advise, mentor, mediate. I also strongly believed in empowering my team members to be as self-sufficient as possible; learned helplessness might make a leader feel important but it doesn't develop any competency in the people.

Recently a former staffer reminded me of a story from when she was a young rep on my team. She recalled, "I kept changing times for meetings, phone calls, appointments with you. After the second or third time, you simply said, 'You are disrespecting my time. Stick with the appointment, or I'll cancel the meeting.' That made a profound impact on the way I showed up with everyone—peers, customers, friends—and how I mother my kids today and lead my own teams. You can be supportive, loving, and firm at the same time."

As the saying goes, be the change you want to see. It starts at the top.

# Moonshine Mondays

*"Happiness is only real when shared."*

ALEXANDER SUPERTRAMP,
A.K.A. CHRISTOPHER MCCANDLESS

I N THE SPRING of 2014, I decided to get back to performing my own songs, which I hadn't really done since the early '90s, at open mics around Toronto. Since 2001, my live gig focus had been on producing, hosting, and performing our Buckley tribute shows between 2001 and 2010, and playing at the annual Chicago events.

I had finally recorded an original album, during 2004–2005, with my friend Mike Borkosky, but I hadn't played any gigs. I was curiously reticent to put together a band and play the songs live. Although I had finally begun to believe I was a good songwriter, I maintained serious self-doubt about performing my own songs. It was one thing to play someone else's tunes, but an entirely different emotional roller coaster to play your own. Nonetheless, I had decided to get back on the horse.

I live in Oakville, about twenty minutes from downtown Toronto. That week in April, I didn't feel like driving downtown to the usual open mics, so I scoped out a small local joint that hosted jams, open mics, and original bands. I had only been to the Moonshine Café once before.

John and Jane, who run the venue, have made a fierce commitment to live, mostly original music. There are no TVs, no pool tables, and a very simple menu. It is all about live music, six or seven nights a week. Local, international, beginners, revered celebrities. It is a haven for many.

That Saturday afternoon, I checked their calendar and it said, "Open Jam @ 3 p.m." It was just after lunch, so I grabbed my guitar and my song notes and figured out what I would play. When I got to the venue, there was a guy in a cowboy hat standing outside next to a barbecue, having a smoke. We exchanged heys. I walked in. Aside from two guys having a quiet conversation, the place was empty and silent.

I asked to no one in particular, "Is there a jam here today?"

"Yeah, go ahead!" one of the men said, gesturing to the stage.

I was about to turn around and leave, disappointed. And then I thought, "What the hell, I'm here. I'll play a few tunes and go home."

I plugged in, adjusted the mic. Played a song. The audience now included the cowboy hat guy from outside. They clapped. "Play another one!" So, I did. And a bunch more. Eventually the two guys got up and joined me—one bass, another guitar. A few more jammers arrived and joined in. And since I was playing all originals, it certainly was a jam,

*I was curiously reticent to put together a band and play the songs live. Although I had finally begun to believe I was a good songwriter, I maintained serious self-doubt about performing my own songs.*

as they had never heard the tunes before. I played for three hours. I had the time of my life.

Turns out the guy in the cowboy hat was John Marlatt, the owner. As I was getting ready to leave, he asked, "Do you want to host a jam night here on Mondays, once a month? We have other Monday night hosts; they rotate through."

Startled, I asked, "What time? I don't stay up late on Mondays. And I don't know a lot of covers. Can I play my own songs?"

"Nine to twelve, leave when you want. Originals are fine. You want to?"

I said yes.

I said my goodbyes, walked out to my car, and thought, "What have I just committed myself to?" And I also thought, "Well, well, well. You wanted to book some original gigs. You now have twelve planned for the next year."

I have hosted there for six years. It has become such a special hub for me, my external living room. I love all the people I have met and befriended, the parties we have had, and making music with others. That is the ticket. Creating music with other people. Beautiful.

I am terribly concerned about the Moonshine Café and the many live music venues around the world, as we continue through this COVID-19 journey. Not only is there a great loss of livelihood to the venue owners and the professional musicians, but the loss of community for all of us who love gathering in spaces where people make music together. Yes, we will pivot, but this is tough.

# Influencing
# Others

*"The objective of debate should be progress, not victory."*

JOSEPH JOUBERT

**W**E KNOW THAT old saying, "You can lead a horse to water, but you can't make him drink." What about helping him realize he's thirsty? This simple statement captures the essence of *influence*.

We often try to control people's behavior—their actions, decisions, agreements—by leading them to the place we want them to be. We direct and cajole, provide logic and data. We want to give the answers and then move on. As leaders and coaches, we want to provide solutions to our employees' and clients' problems. But if we focus on leading them to solutions, we may be missing out on an opportunity to help them identify the true problem.

Consider a different approach: get really curious and help them identify a problem to solve or help them solve it for themselves.

What if we helped the horse focus on his state of being? Is he fully satisfied? Are there any gaps in his physical sense of wellness and health? Once the horse determines, as a matter of fact, he is thirsty, we can lead him through an exploration of how he might solve that problem.

Ultimately one of the solutions is to willingly follow us to the water. It works because he made the decision to act, not us. The decision was based on his own insights and realizations, not on ours. For clients and prospects, this may involve a bit of digging—ask the right questions and help them identify the issues that are underlying the problem they perceive. Help them realize that they are thirsty for a learning culture to improve business outcomes, or to increase agility and collaboration on their teams.

Much work has been done on the power of persuasion—selling skills, negotiation skills, relationship skills, diplomacy—and it all revolves around one's ability to meaningfully connect with another and gently or overtly influence their direction. Focusing the dialogue on uncovering an unmet need is the best way to agree that a solution is required, and then you work together to explore options.

As Daniel Pink articulated in his book *Drive: The Surprising Truth About What Motivates Us*, people are motivated by three primary drivers: autonomy, mastery, and relevance. The notion of making up our own minds is a powerful incentive.

I know that I am far more motivated and energized to do something when I have a sense of agency. That is, I understand its connectivity to something that matters to me; I have a say in how I go about making it happen; and I feel like I'm leveraging or improving my skills, knowledge,

_Consider a different approach: get really curious and help them identify a problem to solve or help them solve it for themselves._

# MASLOW'S
# HIERARCHY OF NEEDS

**Self-Actualization**
Desire to become
the most one can be

**Esteem**
Respect, recognition,
strength, freedom

**Love/Belonging**
Connection: family,
friends, community

**Safety**
Personal security, health,
employment, resources

**Physiological**
Air, water, food, shelter, reproduction

**Note:** We do not experience this in a fixed, linear way.
Depending on different situations and variables, one can
move up, down, and across these needs and express
them in many ways. It's pretty cool stuff to investigate.
If you are so inclined, get curious and check into it.

or service to something or someone. Surely we can all relate to that feeling of having made a difference at the end of a day or a project. That we did something. That we made something. That we served someone or a community. This approach has certainly guided my approach to parenting.

Maslow identified the hierarchy of needs, and it has been proven that once the basic needs are fulfilled—physiological, safety, love—we look for social fulfillment, increased esteem (being respected), and then progress toward self-actualization.

Personally I have found it really interesting to notice when I have been struggling to find myself, to stay focused on learning, expanding, evolving toward self-actualization. In retrospect, I can look back on those times and clearly identify that my basic needs were not being met, and it kept me stuck in the lower parts of the triangle, stuck in fight or flight. When my psychological needs were not met, I simply could not advance to the next stage. Now I am more aware of any niggling feelings that alert me to that reality: where do I need to support myself—or ask for support—to enable my well-being and thus any potential for fulfillment, esteem, and actualization? That is, to live life to the fullest.

In *Your Brain at Work*, David Rock explains the research into our specific brain activity when we perceive choice—which is very different from conditioned apathy when we don't have choice. Research with rats, monkeys, dogs, and yes, humans has shown that there is an inherent need to feel we have choice. Without it, we become apathetic and despondent, and even put our own well-being at risk. To continue with the equine metaphor, the mule digs in its hooves.

To influence effectively, it is critical that the other person knows that the decision to act is entirely their own. They have a choice. It is also important to note the value you provide in distilling the options and facilitating: this creates ease for someone to move toward a solution, instead of being paralyzed by the overwhelming array of choices.

I have had to learn (and continue to relearn) that in order for me to influence others, I must meet them where they are, speak to what matters to them (not to me), and then give them the time and space to determine what steps they want to take (or not!). The more I try to convince, the less I enable us to move closer to mutual understanding.

One of the most effective ways to influence another person, at work or at home, is to enable them to arrive at their own insights when faced with a goal, challenge, or issue. We can advise, direct, or mentor when subject matter expertise and experience is needed.

However, the majority of the time, the most impactful interaction happens when one leads the other through their own exploration of needs, wants, and barriers. And what is exploration but a curious approach to discovery?

The power of that process and the ultimate conclusion and associated action steps, once committed to, is far

greater than the traditional how-to guide to success. This process drives accountability to the choice and increases the likelihood of successful outcomes.

The next time you are frustrated by a client, employee, spouse, child, or peer and you want to tell them what to do to make it better, remember the horse. Leverage curiosity to help him realize he's thirsty and how much he wants a drink of water. He will willingly follow you. Or perhaps he'll lead you both to an even better oasis, yet undiscovered.

 **REFLECTIONS**

Where might you be trying to convince someone or steer something?

How might you begin to use curiosity to ask questions and enable progress, transformation?

Where can you just let it go?

# Grow More, Know More, and Flow More

*"You must go through the way in which you are not.*

*And what you do not know is the only thing you know…*

*In my end is my beginning."*

T.S. ELIOT,
*FOUR QUARTETS*

N REFLECTING ON my curious nature, and how I have an insatiable yearning to understand the why, it strikes me that it might in part be due to the fact that I like to have control over my environment. Perhaps in constantly seeking to understand why, I am seeking some level of certainty, which is clearly the opposite of my previously mentioned favorite Deepak Chopra quote, "Uncertainty is your path to freedom."

And here is the control conundrum: if uncertainty is your path to freedom, and certainty is your path to comfort, it's kind of important that we get curious about what we can control and what we can't control.

If you are being genuinely curious, you are relinquishing control. Control of the outcomes; control of others' responses, reactions, opinions, feelings, and judgments. You are opening up to vulnerability and cultivating an openness in which knowledge, growth, and expansion can flourish.

With these two opposing forces within us, we need to consciously strive to keep one channel open and to be aware of the easy slide back into the second. One of the most basic human needs is for certainty. However, we can separate the human need for certainty in terms of safety and basic physiological needs from the certainty of knowing how everything should play out.

So, this is interesting to me to notice that on the one hand, curiosity does in fact drive me to learn more, to grow more, to know more, to do more, to explore more, and to achieve more. And on the other hand, curiosity is a tool that serves me in gaining comfort and control through growing knowledge. Understanding deeply, completely, unambiguously the "What is going on here?" so that I can feel safe within the confines of the current situation. Even the certainty of "I don't actually know and that's okay too" is comforting if coupled with curiosity. Who knows how this might play out! Regardless, I will learn.

It's important to note that many social and cultural norms and injustices keep people trapped in the fight for basic needs. This whole conversation is moot if we collectively don't expose these toxic norms (gender inequality, socioeconomic and health inequality, food insecurity, racism) and pressure the powers that be to change (tough, as they are the ones who benefit by keeping status quo).

Wow, life is complex and simple at the same time.

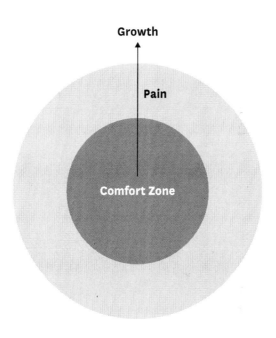

## ◎ REFLECTIONS

How might you begin to notice what's within your control and what choices you have?

How might you begin to notice what you can't control and what choices you have?

Consider three areas in your life where you could release the need for certainty and explore them with a more curious and open mind. For each identified area, reflect on the following:

If you released the need for certainty, how might you benefit? How might you benefit others?

What can you do or put in place to support you having certainty in other areas of your life in order to offset the uncertainty and freedom you experience elsewhere?

*"There are two ways to live your life. One is as though nothing is a miracle. The other is as though everything is a miracle."*

ATTRIBUTED TO

ALBERT EINSTEIN

### "Einstein Was Right"

There are days when the Universe
Speaks to me in song and verse
When everything fills time and space
And there you are with that smile upon your face

You are the sun, miracles everywhere
Einstein was right when he said, it's your call.

There are days when all the rules
Seem so absurd, and guided by fools
And yet you listen to the sages and the seers
And live a lie, fueled by your fears

 catherineharrison.com

# Metaphysics, Reiki, Meditation, Walking

*"Amid the din of the world there are many who yearn for a handful of silence. A silence in which we can take root and grow."*

MARK ROTHKO

WALK ALMOST EVERY day. It helps that I have a young dog that needs to walk a couple times a day. Man, it is a salvation. I walk, and think, and create, and muse, and talk to myself, and sometimes to others. I use it to defrag my mental chatter and get better at noticing.

Movement is energy. Energy is everywhere. We are all connected. Yes, I'm getting metaphysical here, and why not?

In 2012–13, I had added reiki as part of my healing regime. A dear friend was a practitioner, I was going through a tough time, and I thought, "Why not?" It helped. Fast-forward another year, and I decided to take a reiki course—to learn *how* to practice reiki, an energy-healing practice. If I liked the effects of the treatment, why not learn more about how to provide the healing energy to myself and others, individually or collectively. Curiosity led me to seek out a local teacher, to sign up for and complete the coursework to become a reiki practitioner.

My experience was mind-blowing. Imagery, sensations, the connection to those giving/receiving energy—afterward, we would often compare experiences and find that they were identical! I started offering reiki to anyone who wanted it. I decided not to monetize the work, as there are plenty of highly qualified full-time practitioners, but it was an interesting experience to understand what they did, how they did it, what it felt like to give/receive, to be a conduit for the energy available to us all. If you're interested in learning about energy, quantum physics (mind-blowing), or something woo-woo, go for it! Be curious! Where's the harm? I have found it useful and very interesting from an experiential perspective.

In early 2019, I had another concussion that forced me to be quiet and alone for a few weeks. This was my third concussion, with associated whiplash, in six years! A family hockey game was the first one; hitting my head on a heavy beam at a cottage was the second; and the third was a ski accident. The cumulative negative effect on an adult (especially forty-year-old-plus) brain is significant, and I made an explicit and firm decision to put my health, and my brain health, at the top of my priority list. I immediately stopped drinking alcohol. I recommitted to an early-to-rise, early-to-bed routine. I got new reading glasses, as the concussion had changed my vision and I didn't want to add more strain to my wounded brain.

My focus on brain health also triggered a rekindled interest in meditation. Meditation has popped in and out

of my life over the past thirty years (since I was in Nepal in 1992). I wanted the brain healing, clarity, concentration, and stress management that it could bring. It seemed a common-sense choice to reintroduce it to my bucket of healthy habits. Neuroscientific evidence has been particularly vigorous over the past few years in terms of the true physiologic, psychological, and emotional impact that meditation has on the human brain and body.

Randomized studies have shown that new meditators benefit from as little as four weeks of training in the areas

*I don't talk about reiki or quantum theory or living alcohol-free or meditation during my consulting engagements. However, it is part of my philosophy that whole human beings show up in the workplace, and that energy is a palpable, transferrable, meaningful aspect to consider.*

of concentration and emotion regulation. More recent research, using fMRI machines, demonstrates the ability to up-regulate positive emotion, which involves different neural pathways, including activating the dopamine system without external cues or rewards. Incredible! I had nothing to lose.

For the previous year or so, I had been a regular listener of the *Ten Percent Happier* podcast with Dan Harris, in which, although the focus is meditation, the content of the conversations is vast and varied. Harris chats with guests from all walks of life with various peripheral interests, professional expertise, spiritual disciplines, and life stories. In the fall of 2018, there was an episode featuring Jeff Warren, whom I learned was based in Toronto. Warren wrote a book called *The Head Trip*. On the podcast, he had a real, simple way of contextualizing meditation practice that resonated with me, which was aligned with my personal and professional philosophy to connect, create, communicate. Warren was all about keeping it simple and noticing the whole human, with all our messy, kooky idiosyncrasies.

It took only a few minutes for me to find a session with Warren in Toronto. I booked it on the spot, and I attended a How to Guide Meditation workshop—a two-and-a-half-day retreat to kick off my renewed commitment to meditation. The focus was on practicing mindfulness and gaining more clarity, concentration, and equanimity. I have since begun integrating these elements into my personal and professional activities.

These practices are certainly not part of my corporate life. I don't talk about reiki or quantum theory or living alcohol-free or meditation during my consulting engagements. However, it is part of my philosophy that whole human beings show up in the workplace, and that energy is a palpable, transferrable, meaningful aspect to consider. Everyone can relate to feeling good or bad energy. Connecting to your innate, intuitive sense of "What's going on here?" is a valuable human ability.

Sometimes I invite my corporate clients to take a moment and just get present through a tiny guided meditation. (I don't call it that so they don't freak out.) It sets the stage for more open, curious, present dialogue, and hopefully a more forward-thinking, solution-oriented, creative outcome.

I'm curious to see how all of these practices and approaches will continue to dovetail in the coming years. More and more articles, citing scientifically sound evidence, are appearing in the mainstream business media.

Might corporations and their stakeholders be getting curious about the whole human being and how mindfulness helps productivity and profits? Does it help lead to great innovation, sustainability, and good corporate citizenry? I certainly believe the answer is yes.

## ⊚ REFLECTIONS

So, how might you begin to integrate a bit more clarity and balance in your life?

How might you notice and practice mindfulness in stressful situations? When you begin to do that, what do you notice about the difference in experience?

Can you begin to notice when your mind starts to wander? Can you bring it back to the present, if only for a moment?

Can you begin to notice when you are rushing through life? Are there specific activities or events or times of day that are more rushed than others? Where might you slow down to speed up?

Can you begin to notice when you are not listening, i.e., not just "not talking" but "not thinking" either? Can you notice your judgment more clearly and let it go and listen closely to actually understand?

When incorporating these practices regularly, do you notice a more present, calm, or focused sense of being? How does that help you? How does that help others?

# A Story from Beyond

*"Live with intention. Walk to the edge.
Listen hard. Practice wellness.
Play with abandon. Laugh. Choose with
no regret. Continue to learn.
Appreciate your friends. Do what you love.
Live as if this is all there is."*

MARY ANNE RADMACHER

**D**URING MY CORPORATE head office days, I would frequently have lunch at my dad's place. We'd watch the midday news and chat about current events, the sports updates, and connect. He lived five minutes from my office. It was usually an unplanned event, just a "Hey, I'm coming over, see you in five."

On Monday, May 12, 2008, I was at the office and preparing to spend the next few days in Niagara-on-the-Lake at a leadership conference. Around 12:30, I got in my car and decided to go have lunch with my dad, as it would be the only day that week to do so. I got to the exit of the parking lot, put my left-turn signal on, and waited for traffic to clear.

Then out of nowhere, I got a very clear direction to go straight home. Do not go to Dad's place. Oddly I didn't question it. It was so strong and clear. I flipped the signal to turn right and joined the traffic in the direction of my place, instead of his. "Weird," I thought.

I went home, organized my things, packed up, and headed out of town. I called my dad to check in. No answer. Probably grocery shopping.

Tuesday was a full day at the conference, a cross sector group of women leaders discussing and debating effective leadership and emerging development methodologies. I was the head of L&D at the time, and developing sales leaders was one of my priorities. At the end of the day, we had a quick break and then headed off to a winery for a dinner event. Just as I entered the venue, my cell phone rang. My live-in partner and son were calling from home for our daily connect. He also informed me that my aunt was trying to reach my dad, and could I give her a call?

Turns out, my aunt and uncle had been trying to reach my dad and hadn't been able to. I tried to allay their concerns with the fact that he didn't have an answering machine and was often out running errands. He had his regular rounds: library, butcher, grocery store. I called him myself. No answer.

Fifteen minutes later, my boyfriend called me back. "I'm so sorry to have to tell you this. Your dad died. They found him at home." I was in shock and devastated and lost. One of the conference participants was kind enough to drive me back home in my own car (more than an hour away) and take a taxi back to the event.

The next few weeks and months were standard fare for the grieving of a loved one, so I won't go into the details. But the one detail that I reconnected to was the split-second decision in the car on the Monday afternoon. Based on the coroner's report, had I gone there, I would have been the one to find him. And that would've been even more traumatizing. So, I got the message: don't go there.

The fascinating thing about these woo-woo experiences is that there are more and more scientists willing to acknowledge and accept these things we cannot explain away.

 **REFLECTIONS**

When has something like this happened to you?

How can you become more curious about the experience?

# Boredom and Opportunity

*"There are no uninteresting things,
only uninterested people."*

G.K. CHESTERTON

WHEN I WAS a kid and would say to my mom, "I'm bored!" her most likely response was "Well, find something to do." And I did.

That would involve thinking, creating, surmising, using available resources (or MacGyvering new ones), or even just remaining bored for a while and possibly a bit grumpy. I was forced to reflect, consider, create, explore, connect to my feelings (tired? hungry? lonely?) and lo and behold, I would find something to do.

Sometimes it even meant literally sitting and thinking for a good twenty minutes, "What the heck am I supposed to do?" And it led to creativity and exercise and exploring and innovation and making friends. Sometimes my sister and I would just go on an adventure, like cross-country skiing to the forest a few hundred yards from our house with a backpack of canned beans and fruit.

When I was a kid, I used to geek out and actually do science projects just for fun. Because I was bored. One of my favorites to do was a report on birds.

It went like this: go out to see as many birds as I could, describe them in my notebook, go to the library and find a book on birds, find the birds I saw, draw the birds, color the birds, write a report on what I learned about the birds, staple the report, and show it to my mom. To this day, when I see a red-winged blackbird, it reminds me of my bird reports.

I likely never would have done any of that had I been a kid with an iPhone or an iPad. I likely would have played a video game or binge-watched Netflix. In and of itself those activities are not bad—but they are either passive ingestion of entertainment or active engagement in some-one else's imaginary world, not a world of my own creation.

That's not to say I didn't watch TV. I certainly did—but there was a finite amount to ingest. And then I would get bored. And then I would do something else.

The studies show that this kind of free time, even if it results in "getting up to no good," helps kids learn about risks, rewards, consequences, self-sufficiency, indepen-dence, and more. Kids need free time. So do adults.

I regularly observe adults completely immersed in their devices all the time—waiting in line, on a train or plane, sitting in the park, walking the dog, playing with their kids. Very few people look up and out at the world anymore. Nobody experiences boredom because there is a constant stream of data in the palm of our hands.

On the one hand, we're more connected to the world than ever. We are able to stay in touch with friends, fam-ily, events, and have experiences previously undreamed of. We can find information—check the weather, see the Sahara Desert in a windstorm, watch plants grow with time-lapse video—or create our own high-quality films or record our memories. We are able to connect and organize vast numbers of people to bring awareness and change to important causes. All of this is incredible. Think about video conferencing alone; in *2001: A Space Odyssey*, it seemed so far-fetched that one of the characters could par-ticipate in his daughter's birthday party from space. Now we video-conference all the time! We are able to increase the speed with which we can administer the business of our daily lives—securing credit, paying bills, sending money, buying groceries, launching businesses, and getting educated. All mind-blowing in terms of the ability to make our lives more balanced and less frenetic, all while having more free time for the "good stuff."

On the other hand, do we in fact get more free time? Like, really free? Or are we squandering our boredom equity?

We need to protect our brain white space and make some room for adventure, creativity, reflection, growth, and expansion.

When you ask, "How are you these days?" so many people answer "Busy!" If they were to do a thoughtful investigation of what keeps them so busy, likely they would be able to articulate and quantify the minutes (nay, hours!) that they spend distracted by the technology supposed to make their lives better. These are often the same people who complain of being exhausted and tired and overwhelmed and having "no time." They are squandering their boredom equity.

Reconnecting with solitude can be powerful. Many associate solitude with loneliness, but being alone doesn't have to be lonely—it can create the creative white space I referred to earlier. Henry David Thoreau sought out solitude to write his famous *Walden*, first published in 1854. In it, he describes his life in a cabin removed from civilization, and his revelations and experiences of living in relative solitude and contemplation, and the value solitude brought to his creativity and sense of being alive.

Of course, there is a great deal of privilege in having the ability to do this kind of thing. Who has access to things like solitude, freedom from labor, and having their creative work taken seriously? So, how might we all find even microdoses of these things in our daily lives to support us in reconnecting to our white space?

I don't know a lot of people who take a walk or a run anymore without being connected to a device, having someone else's thoughts being streamed through their minds. Even though being outside engaged in these solitary endeavors is a perfect opportunity to let your mind wander, to give it a cognitive break, to truly revel in your own solitude.

When I chat about this topic and invite others to explore solitude as a means to reap the benefits of presence and creative white space, others often report, "I love being alone! I spend tons of time alone!" What they often mean is they spend time alone while reading, watching YouTube or Netflix, scrolling Facebook/Instagram/Pinterest, or listening to podcasts. Solitude means being with your own thoughts and feelings, not ingesting someone else's. Solitude invites personal reflection. You cannot create without solitude. You cannot get clear on who you are, what you want, and how you might get it without solitude.

Back in the early '90s, I remember reading the now widely known *Flow: The Psychology of Optimal Experience* by Mihaly Csikszentmihalyi, an exploration of happiness and what it means to live a fulfilling life. One of the primary concepts is that we enter a state of flow, which feels effortless and timeless, when we have just the right balance of skill and challenge. It made so much sense to me—as a businessperson, multidisciplinary artist, traveler, insatiable asker of why. We've all been there: immersed in something so deeply and fully that time goes unnoticed.

This doesn't mean shifting *everything* around to carve out vast swaths of time (although, go for it if you can and want to!). Just finding fifteen minutes here and there can provide the benefits of solitude, such as focus and presence. You'll notice what works, what doesn't, and likely reconnect to things that matter to you.

Not long ago, I decided to do a month-long digital declutter. I had just finished reading *Digital Minimalism* by Cal Newport, and it resonated with my innate concerns of being hyperlinked to technology all the time. Even though I only use social media on my laptop to minimize the pings throughout my day (no phone apps), I still noticed a pull to those time-sucking portals while I was at my desk.

Some of Newport's key questions are: Are you using technology or is technology using you? Are you consciously thinking about the intrinsic value you are receiving from a given technology or application? Are you allowing it to distract and clutter your mind? Your creativity? Your deep work?

Of course, he reasons, it's not that technology in and of itself is evil or toxic. (Newport has a PhD in computer science, so he clearly sees the benefit of infinite opportunity that tech provides.) But the lack of thoughtful decision-making around how and when we use it leads to our distracted hyper-busy lives.

---

*Solitude means being
with your own thoughts
and feelings, not ingesting
someone else's.*

---

So, what results did I notice as a result of my digital detox? First and foremost, I noticed a compelling pull to check social media when I didn't feel like doing deep work. I also noticed that after I didn't engage in the vortex of social media for a couple of days, I didn't miss it. In fact, I felt quite liberated. I noticed that I felt more content— that is, I was not regularly, repeatedly comparing myself to others' online selves. I walked more. I journaled more. I called people to talk more. I meditated more. I read more. I organized more. I cleaned more. I wrote songs and played guitar more.

I also noticed that I missed a lot of events—people assume everyone is on social media all the time, so they post event information and assume it will be seen. So, I found a specific value in checking social media in a limited way to see what was going on.

Interestingly, at the end of the month, I went back online. I was far more aware of the pull to scroll. And I noticed the old familiar comparisons creeping back into my psyche. So, I made sure I limited myself to five minutes. Check messages, scroll a bit to see what's going on, step out. For those of you who can't imagine that kind of self-limiting behavior, get thee some social media blockers to do the work for you. Even that might cause some stress and anxiety as you set it up, but that is all a good sign that you need to do it—for your own well-being!

Here are a few of the strategies that worked for me:

1   Set a time limit on social media. Be specific about your objective for logging in.

2   Turn off notifications. Check in during specific times. Accept that our human brains are wired to respond to the pings (hence the engineering of said pings). Nothing will get you out of flow and white space faster than your Pavlovian response to a ping.

3   Make a list of other activities you'd like to do but don't. Instead of scrolling, do one of those.

4   Log your activities for a week and see what you're up to.

5   Notice and record how you feel when you use and don't use technology. What are the real benefits? How can you use online tools even more effectively? How can you eliminate some altogether?

6   What tools are actually cooler in concept than in practice? Delete those apps. Delete as many apps as you can at first, and only reinstall them when you understand the value they bring to you, if any.

7   Find five minutes a day to meditate. Don't know how? Check out the (free) Headspace or the Ten Percent app, or have a look at Jeff Warren's website, and get started.

8   We can't all go to our own Walden Pond, but is there a park nearby? Can you find a tree to sit under? Do you have a few houseplants you can sit with? Light a candle? Look at the sky—day or night—and marvel at its vastness?

Most importantly, learn to recognize when you are using technology because it brings you value and when you gravitate toward it even when there's no clear benefit.

When I finished my digital declutter, I noticed that when I went back to using Facebook, for example, that I got stressed again—a niggling negativity of FOMO (fear of missing out) and of paying attention to what I don't have. I noticed who was doing what, where, and with whom and started to feel jealous of their experiences. I was focusing on lack, not abundance.

When I pushed past those feelings, I realized that most of what I was seeing was advertising—all focused on triggering a need for stuff I don't really need. That was interesting and it solidified my decision to carefully manage my use of these platforms—every few days, check in for ten minutes. That's it. This way I reap the benefits of staying connected with my community but avoid the negative effects of being distracted.

Have you ever seen that YouTube video "Cosmic Eye," designed by astrophysicist Danail, of the woman lying in the park, and the shot zooms out and out and out beyond the park, the city, the country, the continent, the planet? That is one of the most visually profound perspectives I keep coming back to. Do I keep myself stuck in a myopic, highly restricted space? Do I squander my boredom equity by keeping blinders on and staying hyper-busy, hyper-distracted?

An important first step is to spend some time analyzing the following:

During what activities do you experience that flow state?

How might you reconnect to those activities, even in a small way?

How can you make room for them in your life?

What can you do to study the impact of technology in your own life?

What might you do to take more control of your precious time and energy, and own your participation in the attention economy?

# Silliness as Art

*"Do you like green eggs and ham?*
*You do not like them, so you say.*
*Try them! Try them! And you may.*
*Try them and you may, I say."*

D R .   S E U S S

HAVE ALWAYS LOVED Dr. Seuss and his ability to experiment, weave a silly thread through a larger, usually profound story, and draw people, old and young, together.

I made up this poem just for fun as Dr. Katz Soose. Why not? What's the risk?

## "Dr. Katz Soose"

What am I? You ask of me
I am a dog I am a tree
I am not you I am not me
Am I here or am I there?
I am not here but everywhere
I am gazillions, I am one
I am everything, I am none
Do I progress by going back
Do you reveal a hidden track
We see the sky, we see the ground
I am not lost I am not found
I am everything I want,
I am the back I am the front
When you release the burden of,
then you will always be enough.
I am not this I am not that
I wear a funky woolen hat
You may ask "What do you do?" as though
What I do defines my soul
How does this solve the mystery of
Who I am below/above
we need not fret,
we let it go
we seek it all
and yet we know

## ⊚ REFLECTIONS

Try it. Don't edit, just write silly stuff and see if you can make it rhyme.

If you can't, who cares? What else did you learn about yourself?

Is there a different way you like to be creative? Do you play best with words, plants, wood, algebra, food, movement?

Go ahead, play a little. If you don't want to, get curious about what's stopping you.

# Doing Less
# with More

*"To talk little is natural*
*Fierce winds do not blow all morning;*
*A downpour of rain does not last the day.*
*Who does this? Heaven and earth.*
*But these are exaggerated, forced effects,*
*And that is why they cannot be sustained.*
*If heaven and earth cannot*
*sustain a forced action,*
*How much less is man able to do?"*

EXCERPT FROM THE TWENTY-THIRD
VERSE OF THE *TAO TE CHING*

**N**OT TO WAX nostalgic for simpler earlier times (we certainly have many advancements to be thankful for), but in our modern age when many of us have conveniences to make our lives easier, simpler, and more luxurious, we feel more exhausted than ever. (I'm speaking from my cushy, middle-class, white Canadian perspective—day-to-day struggles for millions continue to exist.) Why is that? Well, we can point to the fact that we are both hyper-connected *and* more disconnected than ever.

We are hyper-connected to an endless stream of information that necessitates being on, 24/7. Many people keep their phone on even when they sleep and never actually give their brains a chance to rest. As a society, we are on high alert, ever vigilant, experiencing FOMO all the time. The endless scrolling, scrolling, scrolling... We watch and ingest perfectly curated images and stories of others leading to a relentless comparison to our less-than-perfect selves and lives. Conversely, we fill our minds with horrific images from news, entertainment, and video games. We distract and numb, all the while adding to our fatigue.

Cognitive fatigue is real. The brain is an organ that gets tired and overwhelmed just like other body parts. We need to care for it and be the gatekeepers to the onslaught of unlimited, ceaseless information by carefully considering what we feed it.

Many factors influence our brain health and our ability to manage the onslaught. The food we eat, quality and quantity of sleep, exercise, social relationships, and environmental pollution are all aspects requiring attention. Anything that puts your body or mind in a state of stress can interfere with its optimal functioning, and anything that allows you to tap into the parasympathetic nervous system will benefit you. Increased stress levels result in increased cortisol levels which increase inflammation which increase dis-ease in the body.

Sleep is a basic physiological need, like food, water, and air. Sleeping is a vital part of the foundation for good health and well-being. Sleep deficiency can lead to physical and mental health problems, injuries, loss of productivity, and even a greater risk of death. Sleep deficiency can interfere with all aspects of your life. You might have trouble learning, focusing, and reacting. You might find it hard to judge other people's emotions and reactions. Sleep deficiency also can make you feel frustrated, cranky, or worried. A common myth is that people can learn to get by on little sleep with no negative effects. Research shows that getting enough quality sleep is vital for mental health, physical health, quality of life, and safety.

Sleep deprivation and stress also drain our energy, steal our ability to self-control, and shift the brain into a reward-seeking state. Whatever will make you happy (or give you a "hit") in the moment will become a fixation, as you find yourself craving whatever your brain believes will make you feel better. When you're stressed, you are more likely to reach for your distraction of choice. According to the American Psychological Association, the most common stress-coping strategies are also the least effective ones: drinking alcohol, gambling, smoking, playing video games, surfing the internet, watching TV or movies (for more than two hours). These are *not* the most effective stress-relief strategies. Effective strategies include exercising, praying or meditating, reading, playing or listening to music, spending time with loved ones, getting a massage, stretching, going out for a walk, and being in nature.

Here's a simple tip: to tap into your body's relaxation response, try box (or square) breathing. Inhale for four seconds, hold for four, exhale for four, hold for four. This activates and regulates your autonomic nervous system, which can have many benefits such as lowering your heart rate, regulating your blood pressure, and helping you relax, all of which helps decrease cortisol levels in your body. This can rescue your mind from a state of stress and bring a sense of calm and focus that is more conducive to self-control, focus, or rest.

Psychologist Barry Schwartz wrote about the paradox of choice: the more options we have to choose from, the

*That would be doing less with more. Notice that you just have to move one letter and binge turns into being.*

more difficult it is to make a choice. I think this too leads to our modern state of exhaustion. Just think of trying to choose something to watch on Netflix. If there were twenty titles to choose from, pretty easy. There are hundreds. You can scroll and scroll and be seemingly uninterested in the majority. It's simply overwhelming.

We are not wired to keep in touch with so many people. We evolved to keep in touch with a small circle of people in our community. But we have this overwhelming sense that we need to expand our network and our community of people and stay in touch with them through the superficial connections (social media platforms) all the time. It is mentally, emotionally, and psychologically exhausting.

Consider Dunbar's number: 150 is the theoretical limit for the number of people a human can successfully keep track of in their social circles. Whether you believe it to be accurate or not, it makes sense to me. Not that we can't "connect" with thousands, or millions, through social media or other means; it's not the same thing as having relationships. Somehow there has been a shift in cultural expectation and we are now expected to connect and communicate with hundreds, if not thousands, of people all the time. It is curious to consider it. Try it—take a break from social media. See how you feel. Notice who you miss and who you don't. Consider a spring cleaning of "friends" every once in a while. Get back to your core community.

Diet and exercise are two areas that can often become fanatic and stressful. It seems that every few months, a "proven" good thing has been "disproven" and we're supposed to be doing something else! How can we begin to use curiosity and presence to observe what serves our own well-being? If you are exploring something new, try it, observe it, feel it, note it, and make decisions about it. Integrate it or discard it. Remain nimble, open to change, and get more in touch with your own physiology, how *you* feel and the cause and effect of your choices and habits.

And what about all of the causes that are so important to us? Personally, I feel like I should be doing something about all of them. The environment, raising children in this technology age, rampant misogyny and its impact on all other socio-economic factors, racial injustice and wealth disparity, health and dis-ease issues, the plight of the creatures. Feeling like I should be doing more with my ever-faster progressing life. All of this "should-ing" is exhausting in and of itself. Even my hyper-vigilant approach to waste reduction (single-use plastics, anyone?) becomes so tiring at times that I just say fuck it and give up.

We all know the corporate mantra "do more with less." What if we flip it on its head? Instead of scarcity, what if we focused on abundance? What if we explored how we could do *less with more*? As if we already had more than enough, which many of us actually do. If we take the approach of doing less with more, we can be thoughtful about noticing what we have, and when and how to use it most productively.

We might slow down the frenetic, frenzied pace of life. In the corporate world, most organizations have a robust and very generous health plan for their employees. And yet the same corporations have wild-eyed zombies running around the office because leadership hasn't cultivated an environment where rest and sleep is honored as the vital ingredient to human health that it is.

As a business consultant, I often work with companies that have vast inventories of elegantly curated content for meetings, processes, engagement activities. And yet they want more. It's okay to use what you've got. Use it up! Reduce, reuse, recycle can be applied in every aspect of our current single-use disposable culture.

What if we decided to do less with all that we have, that is do less with more? What if we decided to work out less? (Gasp!) I don't mean move less. I mean the hardcore work-out kind of exercise. What if we did less obligatory socializing? What if we put our kids in fewer programs? What if we redecorated our houses less often? What if we shopped less? What if we watched less TV, less Netflix? What if we did less?

What if we cultivated space and time for reflection? What if we got off the hamster wheel of "never enough" and really appreciated all that we have?

That would be doing less with more. Notice that you just have to move one letter and binge turns into being.

## REFLECTIONS

Where in your life are you investing too much of yourself? (No judgment here, just get curious.)

What do you actually do with your time?

When do you do those things?

Who do you do them with?

Who do you do them for?

How might you make adjustments to increase your peace of mind?

Is your behavior in line with your values? How do you know?

# Politics

*"The narcissistic, un-empathic way of being has become so normalized… Where did connection go? Where did 'you are my brother or sister' go?"*

ALANIS MORISSETTE

CAN YOU IMAGINE if everyone (or even just the majority) was curious about political issues?

If we asked more questions, tried to understand different perspectives, tried to understand the storytelling, the patterns, the fear, the opportunities for empathy and collaboration? Imagine if people moved away from the rigidity of partisan politics and toward solving the real issues together, in lieu of pointing fingers and holding fast to opinions. Imagine if we consciously decided to challenge our tendencies toward binary thinking, implicit biases, like-minded circles, and staying comfortable.

Just imagine. Imagination is all about curiosity, open-mindedness.

No further statements, your honor.

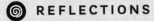

## ◉ REFLECTIONS

Sing John Lennon's "Imagine" right now.

If you don't know it, Google the lyrics.

What does it bring to mind?

What do you like about it? What do you dislike about it? Why?

Is there another song that you really connect to when you think "big world" stuff? Why?

## "There's a Way"

There's a house made out of stone,
No one lives there, no one cares
The ghosts all shake their heads, it didn't have
to be this way
There's no water in the sea,
There's no mountain on the range
Goddess Gaia's had enough, but we don't really
want to change
But there's a way to make it all better
And there's a place we can all come together
The planes fly overhead
And the rockets flaunt their fires
The mothers mourn the dead, and on and on
it goes for years
No one listens, no one learns
No one changes, no one tries
We're expecting everything from the same old sexy lies
But there's a way to make it all better
And there's a place we can all come together

 catherineharrison.com

# Curiosity Is Your
# Path to Deepak

*"Uncertainty is your path to freedom."*

DEEPAK CHOPRA

BACK TO MY Deepak story, which I promised at the beginning of this book. When I was working in pharma, we used to go to lots of amazing places for sales meetings and product launches and conferences. One such sales meeting was at a business conference center in La Jolla, California. It was beautiful and sprawling and connected to a world-class golf course and spa. I was there for a few days. We had a free afternoon on the Wednesday where we could sign up for various paid activities. You could golf, go to the spa, go shopping at some fancy outdoor mall, take a walking trip to the beach. I thought I would just wander the premises, read, and then maybe have a long nap. At the end of our conference sessions on Tuesday, I noticed that adjacent to the business conference center was the Deepak Chopra Wellness Center. "Okay," I said to myself, "let's check that out."

I inquired about Wednesday afternoon. They said they currently had a retreat in session, but there would be an open public meditation, where a handful of other people could join in for a few hours. I thought that sounded interesting and immediately registered. The next day, I finished the morning meetings, grabbed a quick lunch, said see ya to my colleagues, and walked across the parking lot to the center.

I signed in and was directed to a quiet, bright, calm room where there were a bunch of chairs in semicircles. The demographic was a mix of men and women, all ages and ethnicities, no easily defined "meditator types." Participants entered and sat quietly, smiling at each other, waiting for something to happen. Most of the individuals knew each other from the weeklong retreat they were attending. They sat together, chatting quietly. The session leader arrived and began debriefing the key takeaways from the retreat thus far. Individuals shared their personal experiences and aha moments. They welcomed the handful of us who were auditing the afternoon session. There were about twenty of us. The quiet, calm, light energy in the room was a nice antidote to the frenetic pace of the business conference.

After about an hour, in through the side door came a man I recognized. It was Deepak Chopra! He just wandered in, said hi to the teacher, and greeted us in a very casual informal way—"Hey guys, how's it going?" I guess for some of the people in the retreat they were pleased but not surprised that he was there. For me, I was like, "Um, OMG it's Deepak, the 'uncertainty is your path to freedom' guy." Anyway, he asked if it would be cool if he shared

*The demographic was a mix of men and women, all ages and ethnicities, no easily defined "meditator types." Participants entered and sat quietly, smiling at each other, waiting for something to happen.*

with us a presentation he was working on for an upcoming conference. It primarily showed data on the impact of meditation on the brain. Trained as both a Western medical doctor and an Eastern, Indian meditation/spirituality seeker, he was interested in the intersection of these two perspectives—as was I! He proceeded to show us a slide deck that he would be presenting at Harvard University the following week. He led us in an exploration of what we noticed, answered questions, and discussed the content.

What I immediately realized was this: I'm at a pharma medical conference and now I'm listening to Deepak Chopra talk about the scientific study of meditation on our brains and the necessity to blend Eastern and Western practices toward optimal well-being. This. Is. Awesome.

To round up the session, he recommended we meditate together and practice a little exercise he had described. What? Meditate with Deepak Chopra? Yes, please!

It was a simple invitation to get present with the physicality of our hands, however and wherever they were resting. To feel the weight of them resting in our laps, or within each other. And in that few minutes of mindfulness meditation, I noticed both a greater connection to my physical body and also a disconnection from it. That is, I became an observer of the body from that mystical place within. (This kind of practice continues to be a powerful tool I use to ground myself, get present, and slow down when life gets harried.)

Afterward I met a really interesting woman from California. We sat together under a tree and drank tea and talked about life and energy and choices and balance for a couple of hours. And then I went back to my conference for the dinner session and listened to people talk about their golf games and their spa days and their shopping trips and I thought, "Man, you got nothing on me."

LAST THING—thanks for reading this little collection of musings.

What are you curious about now?
Where will you go from here?
What is your very next step?

My goal for myself is to stay safe, healthy, calm, focused, activated, serving others. My goal is to remain curious about what it is, what it might be, what I know, and what I don't know. To stay curious enough to learn everything I can and to share it with those who want to stay curious too.

THERE IS A TAOIST story of an old farmer who had worked his crops for many years. One day his horse ran away. Upon hearing the news, his neighbors came to visit. "Such bad luck," they said sympathetically. "Maybe," the old farmer replied.

The next morning the horse returned, bringing with it three other wild horses. "How wonderful," the neighbors exclaimed. "Maybe," replied the old farmer.

The following day, his son tried to ride one of the untamed horses, was thrown, and broke his leg. The neighbors again came to offer their sympathy on his misfortune. "Maybe," answered the old farmer.

The day after, military officials came to the village to draft young men into the army. Seeing that the son's leg was broken, they passed him by. The neighbors congratulated the farmer on how well things had turned out. "Maybe," said the old farmer.

*Because you just never know.*

# Acknowledgments

I HAD NO IDEA that publishing a book and getting it out into the world would be such a laborious experience! I thought you just wrote a book, printed it, bound it, and put it out there, easy-peasy! Not so fast, Harrison. It takes a village.

Thanks to all my genetic peeps—mom Sandra, sister Liz, niece Hannah, aunt Barb—for your feedback on early renditions. Mom, you especially have been a stalwart supporter and champion of my efforts; thank you for being you.

Thanks to my dear friends Gary Taylor and Michael Darmody for reviewing the first draft of the manuscript and giving generously of your support, love, and terrific input. To Weijia Zhang and his younger, no-nonsense, engineering filter for providing a broader perspective on a non-linear collection of stories.

Thanks to my cousin Kevin Beesley who hooked me up with Jesse Finkelstein at Page Two Books. That initial chat led to a wonderful collaboration.

Thanks to the whole crew at Page Two Books who helped me navigate this new world of publishing. What a great group of humans. Jesse, matchmaker extraordinaire—Emily Schultz as editor was the ticket. If the borders had been open, I would've been hanging out with her in Brooklyn in no time. She pushed me to go deeper, tell more, and refine the narrative. Gabrielle, Chris, Taysia, Crissy, Rony, Jessica, Lorraine, Deanna for all your assistance and support. Who knew a "u" could cause so much debate!

Thanks to my friends Todd Attridge and Erin Somerleigh who helped me with many of the tiny, niggling revisions of peripheral stuff as we were going to print. Todd and Emily also talked me through episodes of massive self-doubt as we got closer to "hitting send."

Thanks to Jeff Buckley. From a tiny bar in Vancouver (and for wearing a Leafs jersey that night), you impacted my life in myriad ways for decades. Thank you Mary—I'm so glad you are in my life. Thank you Andy Ackland for inviting me to go that night.

Thanks to all the people who help me connect, create, and communicate through this process called life, and all the people I've met, interacted with, listened to, watched, and read over the decades who have helped shape my perspective. Some of you have been silent and powerful mentors to me. Others have been in-your-face catalysts that needed to happen to enable my own growth.

Thank you to everyone who offered their kind words and generous praise in support of this project. It means the world to me.

To all the leaders out there: it's hard leading people and it's even harder staying connected to your humanness at the same time. Do it anyway. Keep learning, open your heart and mind, really connect with your people. You'll benefit greatly from it, and so will your business.

As always, the primary nod is to my best creation yet: the kid, ML. Being your mom makes me consistently strive to be a better human. Love you.

**Pandemic work outfit:** Sunday on the bottom, Monday on the top.

# About the Author

CATHERINE HARRISON is the founder and president of Purple Voodoo, a performance and behavior change company that helps individuals and organizations adapt, perform, and thrive. She is a certified professional coach, behavior change specialist, expert facilitator, seasoned team leader, and strategic connector of dots. She is a songwriter/musician, author, painter, environmentalist, and mother based in Toronto. For six years she's been the host of the Cat Jam at the Moonshine Café in Oakville. She has decades of experience as both a corporate professional and a multi-disciplinary artist. *Three Colors, Twelve Notes* is her first book.

# Thanks for investing your precious time and energy in reading my book!

F YOU'D LIKE to keep the conversation going, see full-color images, hear songs from the book, get access to further reflection tools, or book an author event, please connect with me at **catherineharrison.com**.

*Be well and stay curious!*

*Catherine*